Text Processing

ALGORITHMS, LANGUAGES, AND APPLICATIONS

TEXT PROCESSING

ALGORITHMS, LANGUAGES, AND APPLICATIONS

Allen B. Tucker, Jr.

COMPUTER SCIENCE PROGRAM
GEORGETOWN UNIVERSITY
WASHINGTON, D.C.

ACADEMIC PRESS

A Subsidiary of Harcourt Brace Jovanovich, Publishers

New York   London   Toronto   Sydney   San Francisco

ACADEMIC PRESS, INC.
111 Fifth Avenue, New York, New York 10003

United Kingdom Edition published by
ACADEMIC PRESS, INC. (LONDON) LTD.
24/28 Oval Road, London NW1 7DX

Library of Congress Cataloging in Publication Data

Tucker, Allen B
    Text processing.

    (Computer science and applied mathematics)
    Bibliography: p.
    Includes index.
    1. Linguistics––Data processing. 2. Information
storage and retrieval systems. I. Title.
P98.T8   410'.28'542   79–23130
ISBN 0–12–702550–2

PRINTED IN THE UNITED STATES OF AMERICA

79 80 81 82   9 8 7 6 5 4 3 2 1

To my parents

Contents

Preface

Adaptation of the computer for handling natural language text has become one of the most dynamic areas of computer science in recent years. Research in machine translation, content analysis, speech recognition and synthesis, "word processing systems," interactive text editing, and automatic formatting of manuscripts has produced many new and practical uses for the computer.

Accordingly, a growing number of universities have recently begun to offer academic courses in text processing. These courses are especially suited for students in the humanities (as well as in computer science itself) who have practical use for such text processing "tools" as concordance generation, bibliographic information retrieval, and the preparation of theses and other papers for publication.

A 1974 survey by John R. Allen, published in *Computers in the Humanities,* identifies the development of computer courses for humanists in North American universities. The survey indicates that most universities offer such a course with a "hands-on" approach to computers, rather than as a philosophical evaluation of computers and their impact on society. That is, the students generally learn about programming and some specific aspects of text processing from the computer's point of view as well as the user's. The survey also finds that "there is still a great need for a satisfactory textbook to introduce the humanist to the computer, give him practical programming in one of the languages and, perhaps, also introduce him to some elementary statistical material which could have practical application in his work."

The purpose of this book is to introduce the computer to persons interested in text processing. The book identifies text processing applications, introduces the elements of computers and programming using the PL/I and SNOBOL programming languages, illustrates the use of packaged programs for text processing, and surveys the literature on text processing languages, packaged programs, and applications in the humanities.

More specifically, the book was written to provide a unified, self-contained introduction to the use of computers, programming languages, packaged programs, and algorithms for text processing. No prior computer experience on the part of the reader is assumed. Written as a text/reference, the book contains numerous examples, questions, and programming exercises in each chapter. The particular languages we have chosen are PL/I and SNOBOL, because of their wide availability and special capabilities for manipulating text. PL/I is taught in Chapter 2 and SNOBOL is taught in Chapter 3. In a course that uses this book, either one may be taught to the exclusion of the other since none of the later chapters depends on them.

In Chapter 1 the student is introduced to the computer, text processing as a general area of computer application, and the notion of an algorithm. A very elementary algorithm is presented there, and its actions are traced so that the student may gain an initial understanding of the step-by-step sequential nature of program execution. Included in the chapter are discussions of character sets and their impact on the computer representation of text, computer input and output media (tape, disk, terminals, etc.), and the capacities and relative speeds of different hardware elements. Thus, from Chapter 1 the student acquires a basic understanding of computer capabilities and limitations, as well as the programming process itself.

Recognizing that many text processing tasks are best accomplished through judicious use of packaged programs rather than programming languages, four specific packages are introduced in Chapter 4 and information is provided on their use. The computer generation of concordances is illustrated via a KWIC program. The development and retrieval of bibliographic information on a computer is illustrated via a package known as FAMULUS. The use of computer terminals for interactive text editing is illustrated with the CMS Editor. Automatic text formatting and index generation in the preparation of manuscripts is demonstrated with a package known as SCRIPT. Together, these packages embody a variety of widely used text processing functions. The reader will also gain an understanding of the difference between such packages and programming languages in terms of their relative cost and usefulness for specific tasks, so that a basis for making intelligent choices can be formed.

In Chapter 5 the book is concluded with a brief literature review and bibliography for text processing. This review should provide the interested reader with enough information to pursue the topics in greater depth and remain informed about ongoing developments in this fast-evolving field.

Answers to selected exercises and three appendixes are also provided. In Appendix A the EBCDIC and ASCII character sets are given. These are the two most widely used computer coding conventions for letters, digits, and other special characters that occur in text. Appendix B provides some additional details concerning the handling of text data on tape and disk for the most common IBM computers. Appendix C is a glossary which lists and briefly describes all of the so-called text processing primitives that are contained in the book. A *text processing primitive* is our denotation for any elementary function (such as text formatting) that can participate in a text processing application (such as manuscript preparation). This glossary provides a convenient cross reference for the primitives by defining them and indicating where they are discussed within Chapters 1–5.

One of the difficulties that always arises when writing a book like this is that it tends to become dependent upon one particular computer and thereby exclude others. Because this author has easiest access to an IBM 370 computer, the reader will find that some of this book tends to be specifically oriented to the 370, notably in some of the PL/I material and most of the material on packaged programs. Although PL/I is available on Burroughs, CDC, DEC, Honeywell, and Univac computers as well, other languages are more widely used on these machines. Furthermore, each one of the packaged programs is implemented on only one species of computer and no others. Thus, to present any reasonable introduction to the use of packaged programs for text processing would require an exclusive commitment to one machine or another. Nevertheless, we have tried to minimize our dependence on one particular machine so that the "universal flavor" of text processing as a discipline would not be lost. For example, the SNOBOL chapter can be covered in place of the PL/I chapter by students who have access to a computer which favors SNOBOL over PL/I.

This book can be used, therefore, as the basic text in a one-semester course. The chapters should be covered in order, and either Chapter 2 or Chapter 3 can be excluded. It may even be desirable to exclude Chapter 2 or 3 on the grounds of insufficient time to cover them both in one semester. We strongly recommend that the literature review of Chapter 5 be supplemented with outside readings selected by the instructor. The particular selection will depend upon the instructor's own interests and the setting in which the course is taught. For example, if the course is taught within linguistics or English curriculum, additional readings in concordance generation, content analysis, or machine translation may be preferred. If, on the other hand, the course is offered as a computer science course, readings on the design of interactive editors and other text processing software may be added instead.

I would like to acknowledge the many persons who have contributed in special ways to the completion of this book: Charlotte Kaufer has managed the typing and editing of the manuscript with help from Stephanie Nebehay and Frances

Thome. Ross MacDonald, Professor of Linguistics at Georgetown, contributed to the book's initial design. Jan Larsen took the photographs that appear in Chapter 1. Finally, my family—Maida, Jenny, Brian, Perry, and little Josh—have given me continual love, support, and blocks of time for writing; their contribution to my work is immeasurable.

Chapter 1

Introduction to Text Processing

In the past several years, computer use has expanded dramatically into areas where its arithmetic skill is not as important as it "nonarithmetic" skill. In these areas, the computer deals principally with *text*—words, phrases, sentences, names, addresses, formulas, etc.—rather than numbers. With this text, the computer can perform many tasks that have traditionally been performed either by hand or not at all. Such tasks include formatting of text on a typed page, searching for a word in a dictionary, and translation of text from one language to another. When performed by computer, these tasks can often be completed more quickly, accurately, and economically than by hand.

This entire range of computer tasks is called *text processing*. The purpose of this book is to introduce the fundamentals of text processing applications from the viewpoint of one who implements them. That is, we shall describe the computer and programming elements that form the foundation of computer text processing capabilities. The reader will see that writing text processing programs is indeed a special challenge.

This book assumes that the reader has no particular background with computers, but is willing to learn about programming. There is no traditional mathematics background required, except a good attitude toward problem-solving (as would be found, for instance, in tackling the Sunday crossword puzzle). The book is organized as a textbook, with examples throughout, exercises at the end of each chapter, and answers to selected exercises at the end of the volume.

1-1   An Overview of Text Processing

New developments in text processing applications are occurring almost daily. Perhaps the most recent publicity has been given to text processing in the business office's clerical function. Generally called *word processing*, this activity includes at least the capabilities to store (magnetically), retrieve, and automatically retype a form letter with full formatting, at a high rate of speed and in multiple copies, each copy having a different addressee at the top. A typical word processing system is pictured in Fig. 1-1.

Word processing systems usually contain a small computer (called a *microcomputer*) that controls its tasks and a magnetic storage medium that holds the text until such time that it is typed or otherwise processed. Figure 1-2 shows a document that was typed and formatted by a word processing system. Note how the words are adjusted to the right margin *(justified)* and consider how long that would take if it were done by hand. This document was type in 25 secs.

In a number of fields, such as medicine and law, the computer is used as a medium for storage and retrieval of bibliographic information. If the title, author, and other information for each publication in a particular field are stored in a computer, then they can be selectively retrieved at a very high rate of speed. Immense amounts of research time can be saved by generating selective bibliographies in this way. This application of text processing is part of an area known as *information retrieval*. An example of such an application is the National Library of Medicine's MEDLINE, which has terminals linked to its centralized computer bibliography from the libraries of almost every medical research facility in the nation. An example of a bibliography printout is shown

Fig. 1-1. A typical word processing system.

   The geographical distribution of research and development activities is a source of increasing interest and concern. We are just beginning to understand the full impact of largescale nation-wide R&D programs of the last decade. The R&D programs have had a profound effect on economic growth and prosperity in the community, state, and region. At every geographic level these activities benefit.

1. Employment, through more jobs and especially through more technical jobs in the areas of science and engineering, with supporting personnel.

2. Business prosperity, through purchases of machinery and equipment, plant facilities and office furniture, office space, etc., and

3. Education, through modernization curricula and a closer alignment between of training and the skills demanded in today's jobs.

   Each community, state, and region has different needs and different resources--manpower, equipment, leadership--to meet these needs. Effective application of science and technology to satisfy national needs must often focus on a variety of applications to the components of national needs, i.e., specific local needs.

Fig. 1-2. Example document typed by a word processing system.

in Fig. 1-3. Here, the terminal operator had requested a search for references within the category "school phobia."

The analysis and synthesis of natural language by computer has been effectively applied in areas such as automatic generation of indexes for books, machine translation, and content analysis. An example of machine translation from Spanish to English is shown in Fig. 1-4.

Although these systems are often complex and take many years to develop,

```
                 5
AN 77239229. 7711.
AU CRETEKOS C J.
TI SOME TECHNIQUES IN REHABILITATING THE SCHOOL PHOBIC ADOLESCENT.
SO ADOLESCENCE. 12. 46. P237-46. SUMMER 77.

                 6
AN 77193715. 7709.
AU DAVIS J.
TI SCHOOL PHOBIA IN ADOLESCENCE.
SO NURS MIRROR. 144. 17. P61. 28 APR 77.

                 7
AN 77123337. 7706.
AU CONNELL H M.
TI SCHOOL FAILURE-SCHOOL REFUSAL.
SO MED J AUST. 1. 3. P67-9. 15 JAN 77.

                 8
AN 76166787. 7608.
AU LAWLOR E D.
TI HYPNOTIC INTERVENTION WITH "SCHOOL PHOBIC) CHILDREN.
SO INT J CLIN EXP HYPN. 24. 2. P74-86. APR 76.
```

Fig. 1-3. An example of a bibliography printout from MEDLINE.

EN RESUMEN , EL INSTITUTO COLABORA CON LOS PAISES EN RELACION CON EL DIAGNOSTICO DE LA SITUACION NUTRICIONAL Y ALIMENTARIA ; LA INTEGRACION DE LA NUTRICION EN LOS PROGRAMAS DE SERVICIO DEL SECTOR SALUD ; LA INCORPORACION DE LA ENSENANZA DE LA NUTRICION EN TODOS LOS NIVELES ; LA EDUCACION NUTRICIONAL PARA LA POBLACION GENERAL ; LA ATENCION DE LOS DISTINTOS GRADOS Y FORMAS DE DESNUTRICION ; LOS PROGRAMAS DE ALIMENTACION SUPLEMENTARIA Y DE ORGANIZACION Y FUNCIONAMIENTO DE SERVICIOS DIETETICOS DE HOSPITALES Y OTRAS INSTITUCIONES .

IN SUMMARY , THE INSTITUTE WORKS WITH THE COUNTRIES IN RELATION TO THE DIAGNOSIS OF THE FOOD AND NUTRITIONAL SITUATION ; THE INTEGRATION OF THE NUTRITION IN THE PROGRAMS OF SERVICE OF THE HEALTH SECTOR ; THE INCORPORATION OF THE TEACHING OF THE NUTRITION IN ALL THE LEVELS ; THE NUTRITIONAL EDUCATION FOR THE GENERAL PUPULATION ; THE ATTENTION OF THE DIFFERENT DEGREES AND FORMS OF MALNUTRITION ; THE PROGRAMS OF SUPPLEMENTARY FEEDING AND OF ORGANIZATION AND OPERATION OF DIETETIC SERVICES OF HOSPITALS AND ANOTHER INSTITUTIONS .

Fig. 1-4. An example of machine translation from Spanish to English.

they all rely fundamentally on a collection of text processing *primitives*. That is, they contain program elements that accomplish some very fundamental transformations on free-running text. These primitives and program elements will be of central interest in this book. It will be important for us not only to identify these primitives, but also to show how they take part in larger systems of the kind described above.

1-2 Text Processing Primitives

What, then, are the primitive functions that comprise the foundation for these large, complex text processing systems? We identify a small, yet important collection of them here and use this collection as a basis for discussion in later chapters.

(1) *Paragraph formatting and margination.* This primitive's effect is shown in Fig. 1-2. Basically it includes laying out each paragraph on a page so that no word is split between two lines, each line begins in the same tab position (except the first, which is indented), and words are adjusted to the right margin (with spacing inserted between words to compensate).

(2) *Word and phrase identification.* The effect of this primitive is found in the bibliographic print-out in Fig. 1-3. The particular items listed there are extracted from a very large data file on the basis that they contain one or more words and phrases that match with a prescribed list of desired words and phrases.

(3) *Word and phrase sorting.* The sorting, or arranging in alphabetical order, of a series of words and phrases is at the heart of systems that automatically generate indexes from free-running text. Indexes are important tools in language analysis and are a standard component of most textbooks.

(4) *Dictionary search.* Computer translation and/or "understanding" of free-running text requires very extensive dictionaries. The Spanish–English translation shown in Fig. 1-4 requires a dictionary of Spanish terms and equivalent English terms; the program must search the dictionary for each word in the Spanish text that it encounters in order to derive the appropriate English term for the translation. Since the words in the Spanish text occur in nonalphabetical order, the dictionary search itself must be "random." That is, *any* particular word in the dictionary must be *immediately accessible* no matter where it is in the alpabetical ordering of the dictionary.

(5) *Text editing and statistics gathering.* Most text processing systems must provide some facility for reviewing a text after it has been prepared for computer use, and then correcting errors that are encountered. This facility is usually able to *count* the number of units (words, sentences, paragraphs, bibliography entries) in the text, for purposes of control and estimation of future computer requirements for processing.

There are many more functions that can be identified as text processing primitives. We will use these five and others for programming demonstrations and exercises in later chapters. Appendix C contains a glossary of all the test processing primitives that appear in this book, together with a cross reference to their different appearances.

1-3   Programming Languages and Packaged Programs for Text Processing

Our primary interest in this book is to explore how text processing primitives are implemented on computers. Two alternative vehicles are available for such implementations:

(1) programming languages, and
(2) packaged programs.

We discuss the major elements of these two alternatives in the following paragraphs.

The purpose of a programming language is to describe, using terminology, that is understood by both the computer and the programmer alike, exactly *how* a text processing primitive is to be performed by the computer. We shall expand on this concept more fully in the next section and later chapters. To learn a programming language and to master programming techniques requires some effort, since the language is relatively artificial and the computer's repertoire of possible actions is rather limited, in relation to a human's. Once the programming is done, however, a computer can perform a primitive many thousands of times faster and more accurately than can a human.

A large number of programming languages are in use today. Among them, the most widely known are COBOL, FORTRAN, BASIC, and RPG. None of these four, unfortunately, is particularly well-suited for programming text processing problems. COBOL and RPG are designed principally for business data processing problems, such as payroll calculation and accounting. FORTRAN and BASIC are designed principally for mathematical and statistical programs, such as linear programming and regression analysis.

Two languages that are well-suited for text processing problems are PL/I and SNOBOL. We shall teach these languages in Chapters 2 and 3 and use them as our vehicle for programming a number of text processing primitives.

In addition to programming languages, several commercially available "packaged programs" are designed to perform certain widely used text processing primitives. Unlike programming languages, packaged programs allow the individual to select *what* function to perform rather than describe *how* to perform it, in a level of language that is simpler than that of a programming language.

Packaged programs thus relieve the individual from the tedious details of programming.

Although packaged programs are easier to use than programming languages, they are limited by the following two characteristics:

(1) Packaged programs perform only a limited number of primitives, such as "generate an index from a text," and these often cannot be specialized to the particular characteristics of an individual text. By comparison, programming languages are not so limited; the programmer can build any desired primitive for any particular kind of text and, in effect, "package" the program.

(2) Packaged programs are often less efficient than programming languages in their utilization of computer resources.

Nevertheless, packaged programs ought to be used in preference to programming languages whenever possible. Such use eliminates duplication of programming effort.

Like programming languages, a large number of packaged programs are available for text processing. Among these are SCRIPT, FAMULUS, the CMS Editor, and KWIC. SCRIPT is a text editing and formatting package. FAMULUS is a package that can be used for bibliographic information retrieval. The CMS Editor is a package that allows convenient editing and correction of text. KWIC is a package that can be used to generate an index from a running text. We illustrate the use of each of these packages in Chapter 4.

The reader should avoid the temptation to bypass the study of programming languages for text processing in favor of the various packaged programs. After all, the packaged programs have themselves been developed from programming languages at some earlier point in time. Furthermore, many of the text processing primitives that will be studied in the main body of Chapters 2 and 3 are embedded within the packaged programs themselves. That is, the study of programming languages for text processing will not only give the reader a first-hand ability to solve text processing problems in general, but will also demonstrate the complexity and processes that occur within the packages themselves.

1-4 The Algorithmic Approach to Text Processing

When faced with the problem of implementing a text processing primitive we first must understand some basic concepts of computing. That is, a primitive must be built within the context of established computer concepts. In this and the next section, we present these concepts, using a very simple text processing example as a vehicle for discussion. These concepts together should equip the reader with a basic framework within which the programming methods of Chapters 2 and 3 can be developed.

Every program is an example of the general notion of *algorithm*. An algorithm is defined as a precise description (i.e., a prescription) of the individual steps that are required to perform a task. Well-known examples of algorithms are the recipes in a cookbook. Implicit in this definition of an algorithm is the idea that the steps to be carried out are within the capabilities of the performer (i.e., the performer can understand and successfully complete each individual step) and that there is no room for deviation from the prescribed steps. That is, an algorithm is written in such a way that it will be slavishly executed.

As an example, suppose we are asked to describe an algorithm that, for an arbitrarily selected text, will count the number of words in the text. Note that we are *not* asked simply to *count* the words in a text, but moreover we must come up with a *counting procedure*. In order to accomplish this, we must have in mind some fundamental capability to recognize or distinguish an individual word, as well as some ability to mechanically move from one word in the text to the next. Also we must assume that an elementary arithmetic capability exists for counting, and that some capability is present to detect that the end of the text has been reached. In other words, the description of an algorithm is predicated on the existence of some well-defined collection of elementary operations from which it can be built.

Of course, any reasonably skilled human can carry out this task. But our aim is to describe this task in such a way that a machine, or computer, endowed with suitable elementary capabilities can also carry it out. Thus, we must dwell on some apparently trivial matters in order to establish a proper context for describing algorithms.

Thus, we first establish the primitive capabilities themselves. They are typical of those that would be found in an actual computer, and are as follows:

(A)   The computer can establish a counter and set its value to zero. This will be pictured as follows:

$$\boxed{0}$$

(B)   The computer can add 1 to the value of the counter.
(C)   The computer can move from the beginning of one word to the beginning of the next word in the given text.
(D)   The computer can recognize if it is scanning the last word of the text.
(E)   The computer can stop executing on command.

To picture the actions of the computer with respect to a given text, we shall associate with the text a pointer (↑) as follows:

 Each preposition operates syntactically .

Here, the position of the pointer designates that word in the text which the machine is presently "scanning." A "move" is depicted by simply moving the pointer to the beginning of the next word.

The algorithm itself is written as a numbered sequence of imperative instructions, or commands. The instructions are to be serially executed by the computer, beginning with the first, and with the pointer initially positioned before the first word in the text. Under these constraints, and with the primitives given above, we can now describe an algorithm that counts the words in any such text.

Instruction number	Instruction
1	Set the counter to zero.
2	Move to the beginning of the next word.
3	If there is no next word, then stop.
4	Otherwise, add 1 to the counter.
5	Proceed to instruction number 2.

We can see from this simple description that instructions 2-5 will be repeated until the end of the text is scanned. At that time the counter will contain the number of words in the text. For the example text given above, we can "trace" the execution of this algorithm as follows:

Step	Instruction	Text	Counter
1	1	Each preposition operates syntactically .	0
2	2	Each preposition operates syntactically .	
3	3		
4	4		
5	5		1
6	2	Each preposition operates syntactically .	
7	3		
8	4		
9	5		2
10	2	Each preposition operates syntactically .	
11	3		
12	4		
13	5		3
14	2	Each preposition operates syntactically .	

15	3		
16	4		
17	5		4
18	2	Each preposition operates syntactically .	
19	3		
20	4		
21	5		5
22	2		
23	3 (stop)		

When execution stops, therefore, the counter contains the number of words in the text. As the reader will notice, a "word" in this context is any sequence of nonblank characters that is followed by a blank and contains no embedded blanks itself. Thus, the period (.) is just as much a word, in this sense, as any other. We shall discuss in later chapters the means for distinguishing between actual words and other syntactic marks. This is generally not an easy problem in text processing applications.

This illustration embodies several principles of computer programs. First, the text itself that is the subject of analysis is known as the *input*. The algorithm itself is known as the *program,* and the particular language and stylistic conventions in which the algorithm is written are known as the *programming language*. The result (i.e., the final value of the counter) is known as the *output*.

Our definition of algorithm can now be refined to denote any program, written in some well-understood programming language, which has the following functional characteristics:

(1) It performs some well-defined task, for any input text, and leaves the appropriate output.

(2) For any suitable input text, it stops executing after a finite number of steps.

The input for an algorithm is always assumed to be finite in length (although it may be very long). The algorithm, in turn, should be written so that it works properly for any suitable input text. That is, an algorithm should be general.

The input to an algorithm is usually processed in *sequential* manner. That is, the words are scanned from beginning to end, starting with the first and without backing up. If more than one result were to be provided as output by an algorithm, it too would usually be generated in a sequential manner. Nonsequential input and output, in which individual data items (e.g., individual words in a text) are accessed in a *random* order, is also useful in certain special applications. We shall illustrate its use in Chapter 2 when we discuss computer-based dictionary applications.

1-5 Computer Elements for Text Processing: I/O, Storage, and CPU

Section 1-4 introduced some general notions about programs and text processing algorithms. In this section, we describe the computer elements that are used to implement these programs.

1-5.1 Input-Output Media

Before input text can be processed by a program, it must be transcribed into a computer-readable medium, such as punched cards, magnetic tape, or magnetic disk. Transcription to punched cards is accomplished by using a keypunch machine (Fig. 1-5). Transcription to magnetic tape may be done by way of a key-to-tape device. Transcription to magnetic disk may be done by way of an interactive terminal (see Fig. 1-6).

Whichever medium is used, the data are recorded using a fixed, computer-dependent coding scheme. This scheme assumes a specific collection of characters, called the computer's *character set*, in which all text must be encoded. The standard IBM character set for punched cards is shown on the punched card in Fig. 1-7.

More extensive character sets are available when interactive terminals and other media are used for recording data. Especially important to text processing,

Fig. 1-5. A keypunch machine.

Fig. 1-6. An interactive terminal.

for instance, is the availability of lowercase and uppercase letters. These are not available in the character set shown in Fig. 1-7. They are available, however, in the full ASCII and EBCDIC character sets (see Appendix A), which are supplied on many kinds of interactive terminals. Also, a special adaptation of the keypunch machine will permit the keying of these character sets. In general, these three input devices can be operated as ordinary typewriters for the purpose of entering input text into a computer-readable medium.

Compared with other recording media, the punched card has as its main advantage the ability to be easily recorded and manipulated. However, only a

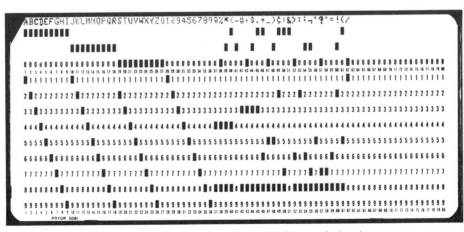

Fig. 1-7. The IBM standard character set in a punched card.

limited quantity of text can be stored in punched cards, since each card accommodates only 80 characters of information. For this reason, magnetic tape or disk is often preferable. A reel of magnetic tape is pictured in Fig. 1-8.

Typically, data are recorded on magnetic tape at a density of 1600 characters per inch, and an average reel is 1200 ft long. However, the data must be grouped into ''blocks,'' which for purposes of electronic reading and writing are mutually separated by a ''gap'' of about ¾ in. The number of characters in each block is governed by the program. It might, for example, be 1600 characters per block. If this is the case, then one block and its adjacent gap occurs on every 1-¾ in. of the tape, as shown schematically in Fig. 1-9. A single reel of tape can thus store more than 8000 1600-character blocks. This is equivalent to more than 160,000 cards. At an average of 10 words per punched card, the capacity of one reel of tape is a text of more than 1.6 million words. Storing such a large text on punched cards would therefore be unmanageable.

Magnetic disk has the same basic advantage over punched cards as magnetic tape, especially when considering large texts. Magnetic disk ''packs'' are shown in Fig. 1-10. Generally, a disk pack's capacity is similar to that of a tape reel. However, disk differs from tape and punched cards in a fundamental way. The

Fig. 1-8. A reel of magnetic tape.

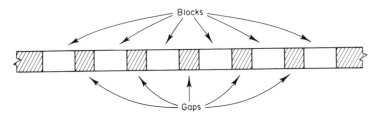

Fig. 1-9. Blocks and gaps on magnetic tape.

data on cards (tape) must be accessed by the program *sequentially,* that is, one card (block) at a time beginning with the first. Data on disk, on the other hand, may be accessed either sequentially or *randomly,* that is, in an order that is unrelated to the physical sequence in which the blocks are stored on the disk. Random access has special value in certain text processing applications, as we shall see in Chapter 2.

However, magnetic disk is also a more expensive medium for storing text than magnetic tape or cards. Thus cards and tape should be viewed as preferable to disk unless the computing task requires random access rather than sequential access.

For output, the most common medium is printed paper. A typical computer's printer is pictured in Fig. 1-11. A printer operates sequentially, printing one line at a time and proceeding down each page. Since the pages are attached by perforation, the end of one page is followed physically and logically (from the viewpoint of the program) by the beginning of the next. Since the printer is a sequential device, it cannot be "backed up" and its lines cannot be randomly selected for output. This places a modest burden on the program for producing printed output in the correct physical sequence, as we illustrate in later chapters.

Other output media include magnetic tape, magnatic disk, terminals, and punched cards. Generally, magnetic disk is used as an intermediate storage

Fig. 1-10. Magnetic disk packs.

Fig. 1-11. A typical printer.

medium when the program is processing large amounts of text, and magnetic tape is used as a final storage medium in such a process. Punched card output has only occasional usefulness.

1-5.2   Storage and CPU

The principal component of a computer is its *central processing unit* or CPU. Here is located the control circuitry for executing programs as well as the memory where the programs and the intermediate counters are kept. A schematic description of the CPU and the various input and output devices is shown in Fig. 1-12.

The control circuitry executes the individual steps of a program in a slavelike manner. If the program, for example, were the one given in Section 1-4, its instructions would be placed in the memory, and the memory would also contain the counter that was used to keep track of the number of words in the text. "Each preposition operates syntactically," would be encoded on a suitable input medium, such as the punched card shown below.

```
EACH PREPOSITION OPERATES SYNTACTICALLY.
```

The output would be the resulting value of the counter, which could, although not specified by the example program, have been displayed on printed paper.

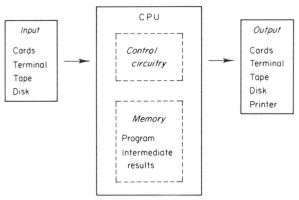

Fig. 1-12. CPU, input, and output relationships.

1-6   Special Considerations for Text Processing

Whether a programming language or a packaged program is used to solve a text processing problem, certain special considerations must be taken into account when implementing that solution. These considerations principally involve the limitations of memory and processing speed, as well as the choice of encoding method for the text itself.

1-6.1   Memory, Speed, and Their Limits

Recalling the diagram of Fig. 1-12, it should be emphasized that the amount of memory in the CPU is available in much more limited supply than the space on a disk pack or magnetic tape. For this reason, most text processing algorithms are designed in such a way that a reasonably small amount of text, such as a single sentence or a single paragraph, is treated as a "unit of analysis." The program proceeds by reading one such unit into memory from the input medium, processing it, perhaps producing intermediate results, and then reading and processing the next unit in the same manner. This approach is further justified by the general computer requirement that no processing of an input text can be done by the program until the text has been transferred from the input medium into memory.

Once the unit of analysis has been transferred into memory, however, processing can be performed at a very high speed. For example, a 100-word text can be rearranged into alphabetical order by a program in a fraction of a second. Thus, the program must try to bring into storage as much text as possible to take advantage of this processing speed, without exceeding the limits of memory itself.

The data capacity of tape or disk is, on the other hand, almost limitless. Yet, the speed of transferring a single sentence of text from tape or disk into memory is measured in thousandths of a second. This is relatively slow compared with a transfer rate measured in millionths of a second, for the same sentence moving from one memory location to another within the CPU. Thus, an optimal text processing program will seek to balance these conflicting limits, the slow speed and high capacity of text input and output media vs. the high speed and low capacity of memory.

The practical implication of these considerations is that programs that minimize their computer time and memory requirements generally cost less (in actual dollars) to run, and may enjoy preferential treatment in scheduling for execution at the computer center. Learn about your own computer center's procedures for scheduling program executions and billing for computer use.

1-6.2   Encoding Conventions for Text

An immediate problem that all text processing applications encounter is the determination of an appropriate encoding convention for representing the particular input text being processed. These conventions vary among different computer species, installations, text processing packages, and programs. They are largely determined by the character sets for the input media (e.g., punched cards, interactive terminals) that are available at the computer center where the program (package) is developed. Encoding conventions are also determined by the particular nature of the text itself: its special characters and the analysis that it will undergo.

Common to most text processing programs is the question of accommodating the fact that the standard 60-character keypunch (Fig. 1-5) does not contain lowercase letters. In this case, some method must be established for distinguishing capital letters from lowercase letters. A simple method is to precede each capitalized word by a specially designated character, such as the vertical bar (|), to deonote that the word is capitalized. A word that is composed of all capital letters can be prefixed by two vertical bars (‖). Thus, for example, the text "Using the IBM 60-character set" can be keypunched as:

|USING THE ‖IBM 60-CHARACTER SET

Another frequent source of difficulty involves the problem of distinguishing between the end-of-sentence period and the period that abbreviates a word (as in Dr.). Worse still, the final period in some sentences serves both purposes, as in the following:

They live in Washington D.C.

A simple convention for distinguishing among these uses of the period is to separate it by at least one space from the last word in the sentence. Thus, for instance, the above sentence would be encoded as follows:

|THEY LIVE IN |WASHINGTON ‖D.C.

Here, the final period denotes the end of the sentence, while the others are attached to the word itself.

Other encoding problems arise when dealing with scientific text and text in a foreign language. In these cases, we encounter symbols that are not closely approximated in standard character sets. Examples include the Greek letters in scientific text, letters of the Cyrillic alphabet in Russian text, and accents in Romance language text. Each of these situations requires the use of special encoding conventions. Figure 1-13 shows a text that contains many of these special symbols. Figure 1-14 shows how it will look after it has been encoded in the 60-character keypunch alphabet, using a special encoding convention.[1]

The rubric EVENT specifies a reference to anything which can be defined in part, if need be, by references to TIME, particularly to the time at which or during which it occurred. The rubric EVENT will be assigned to such signals as

concert, concert, концерт;
began, commença, началось;
revolution, révolution, революция.

Fig. 1-13. A text with special symbols.

$P $S THE RUBRIC $AC EVENT SPECIFIES A REFERENCE TO ANYTHING WHICH CAN BE DEFINED IN PART , IF NEED BE , BY REFERENCES TO $AC TIME , PARTICULARLY TO THE TIME AT WHICH OR DURING WHICH IT OCCURRED . $S THE RUBRIC $AC EVENT WILL BE ASSIGNED TO SUCH SIGNALS AS $M $I CONCERT , $I CONCERT , $CY KONQERT ; $M $I BEGAN , $I COMMENC,A , $CY NACALOS6 ; $M $I REVOLUTION , $I RE1VOLUTION , $CY REVOLHQI4 .

Fig. 1-14. An encoding of that text.

Under this convention, the character $ is used to "escape" from the confines of the limited 60-character alphabet in order to express a feature of the text that is not directly representable in the alphabet itself. The one- or two-character code that follows the $ identifies the feature itself. The reader can see that $P means "begin a new paragraph," $S means "begin a new sentence," $AC means "the word that follows is completely capitalized," $M means "indent to a new margin," $I means "underscore the next word," and $CY means "the next word is an encoding of Cyrillic symbols."

[1] This convention was developed by R. Ross MacDonald, Professor of Linguistics, Georgetown University, Washington, D.C.

Questions and Exercises

1. What is *test processing?*
2. Identify two or three text processing applications with which you are already acquainted.
3. Within one of those applications, can you identify one or more of the text processing primitives that were presented in Section 1-2? Can you identify any primitives in addition to those presented?
4. What are the relative advantages of using a programming language for text processing, as opposed to using a packaged program? Disadvantages?
5. There are several programming languages and text processing packages beyond the ones mentioned in Section 1-3. If you know of any, identify their main applications (if any) in text processing.
6. What is an algorithm?
7. Using the algorithm presented in Section 1-4, trace its execution for each of the following "sentences" as input.
    (a) Go .
    (b) Go to town .
    (c) .
8. Slightly modify the algorithm presented in Section 1-4 so that it counts only the number of occurrences of the word "the" in the sentence. Assume the same primitive capabilities as in the original algorithm, with the additional proviso that the machine can recognize if it is scanning a *particular* word (such as "the") via the following kind of instruction:

    "If the currently scanned word is 'the,' then . . ."

    Here the ellipsis (. . .) indicates one of the machine's other primitive capabilities.
9. Trace the execution of your modified algorithm with each of the following input texts.
    (a) The cat in the hat .
    (b) Each preposition operates syntactically .
    (c) the cat in the hat .
10. What is the meaning of the term *sequential? Random?*
11. Name and discuss the relative merits of three different input media. Output media.
12. (a) For a 1200-ft reel of tape, assuming that data are recorded at a density of 1600 characters per inch, how much of the reel will be filled by the words of a 100,000-word dictionary? Assume that the average word size is 5 characters, there is exactly one blank space (also a character) between each

pair of adjacent words, and that the size of each *block* on the tape is 1000 characters (including blanks).

(b) Perform the same estimate for a block size of 80 characters.

(c) Sometimes tape data are recorded at a density of 6250 characters per inch. Redo the estimates of (a) and (b) under this assumption.

(d) Find out the tape data recording density for your computer installation.

13. Identify the main components of the CPU. What two functions does the memory perform?

14. When designing text processing programs, what characters of input/output media should be kept in mind? What characteristics of memory?

15. In what way does a computer's available character set become a factor in designing text processing applications?

16. Describe briefly the essential elements of the two encoding conventions presented in Section 1-6. Briefly discuss the relative advantages and disadvantages of each for encoding, say, a 100,000-word text.

Chapter 2

Introduction to PL/I for Text Processing

This chapter presents the features of PL/I that are essential to text processing applications. The reader should understand that this is not a complete presentation of PL/I; this language has many features that are used in other applications. Among the text processing primitives that are presented in this chapter, we include a PL/I version of the word-counting algorithm that was introduced in Chapter 1.

All PL/I programs and data must be represented in the so-called PL/I character set, which is as follows:

ƀ (space)
. (+ | & $ *) ;
− / , % _ ? : # @ ' =
A B C D E F G H I J K L M N O P Q R S T U V W X Y Z
0 1 2 3 4 5 6 7 8 9

The reader should verify that this is similar to the EBCDIC character set given in Appendix A.

2-1   Numbers, Strings, and Declarations

When prepared for processing by a PL/I program, data values must fall within one of two elementary categories: arithmetic and string. An arithmetic data value is simply a number, as illustrated by the following examples:

-1.75   0   37   .00025

As we shall see, numbers are used in text processing for a variety of auxiliary purposes. For example, the algorithm of Chapter 1 shows the use of numbers in counting the words in a text.

A string data value is composed of any sequence of characters from the PL/I character set. Whenever it appears within a PL/I program, a string data value must be enclosed between apostrophes ('). Any occurrence of an apostrophe with in the string itself must be denoted by two successive apostrophes (' ') to avoid confusion with the enclosing apostrophes. The following strings illustrate these conventions.

```
'ABC'
'AbBbC'
' '
'WHAT''SbTHIS?'
```

We emphasize that the first two strings are not "equivalent" in any sense; the blank (b̄) is always significant within a character string.

Finally, we note that a character string is said to have a *length*, which is simply its number of characters (excluding the enclosing apostrophes). The four strings above, for example, have lengths of 3, 5, 0, and 12 (not 13!), respectively.

2-1.1   Variables

A PL/I *variable* is the means by which values (i.e., numbers and strings) are stored in the memory. A variable has two parts, a *name* and a *memory location*, which contains a value. We use the following convention throughtout to denote a variable:

```
name   | value |
```

The programmer chooses the name of each variable to be used by the program, and usually chooses one that mnemonically describes its purpose.

For example, we may have a variable whose value is the number of words in a sentence, and another variable whose value is a sentence itself. Appropriately, we may choose to name these variables NWORDS and SENT, respectively. Thus, we have identified the following variables:

```
NWORDS  |        |

SENT    |        |
```

The *value* of a variable may be either a number or a string. However, the value of a variable may change from time to time during the execution of a

program. For example, the value of the variable SENT may at one time be
'EACH PREPOSITION OPERATES SYNTACTICALLY . ' :

SENT | EACHbPREPOSITIONbOPERATESbSYNTACTICALLYb . |

At another time, the value of SENT may be a totally different sentence. Similarly,
the value of NWORDS may be 5 at the time this particular sentence is processed
by the program:

NWORDS | 5 |

In any event, two principal characteristics of variables must be remembered:

(1) A variable can never have more than one value at one time. That value
is assigned by the program itself, and is lost each time the program assigns a
new value to the variable.

(2) A variable may contain either numeric values or string values. This is
determined at the outset by the programmer. For example, the variable NWORDS
above will always contain numeric values (never a string).

To identify the variables that will occur in a program, the PL/I programmer
uses the *declaration*. This statement not only assigns a name to each variable,
but also identifies the type of value that the variable will contain. The basic form
of the delcaration is as follows:[1]

DECLARE   name   type ;

Here, "name" denotes the name of the variable, and "type" denotes the type
of its value (numeric or string). A variable's name may be any sequence of
letters and/or digits, as long as it begins with a letter. Its type denotes the nature
of its value as follows:

Nature of a variable's value	type
Numeric (strictly integer values)	FIXED BINARY
Numeric (decimal numbers)	FIXED DECIMAL (p, q)
String	CHARACTER (n)
	or CHARACTER(n) VARYING

---

[1] To describe the syntax of PL/I declarations and statements, we use uppercase words and other
punctuation to denote required parts and lowercase words to denote varying parts (which are determined by the programmer). When letters of a word are underlined, this denotes an allowable
abbreviation. In the above, for instance, DECLARE may be abbreviated as DCL.

When a variable is used strictly as a *counter*, its value will always be an integer. Such is the case, for instance, with the variable NWORDS described above. Thus, we should declare such variables as:

DECLARE   NWORDS   FIXED   BINARY;

Abbreviated, this can be written as

DCL NWORDS FIXED BIN;

On the other hand, when a variable is used to denote a number that is not necessarily an integer, its type can be of the form FIXED DECIMAL (p, q). Here, p denotes the toal number of significant digits in the variable's largest value, and q the number of decimal degits to be retained. For example, suppose we want to compute the average number of words per sentence, having counted both the total number of words among the sentences of a text and the total number of sentences. We could call this variable AVWORDS, and decide that the desired average will be no greater than 99 and the number of decimal digits retained will be one. That is, the average will be of the form xx.x, where each x denotes a single decimal digit. The following are three possible values for the variable AVWORDS under these assumptions: 12.3, 4.5, 40.0. A declaration for AVWORDS can be written as:

DCL AVWORDS FIXED DEC (3,1);

When a variable's value will be a *string*, its type can be declared as CHARACTER (n) or CHARACTER (n) VARYING. In the first case, any string value that the variable assumes must have the same fixed length, designated by "n." In the second case, any string value that the variable assumes may have a different length but none may have a length greater than "n." For example, reconsider   the   variable   SENT,   and   assume   that   its   value   is 'EACHbPREPOSITIONbOPERATESbSYNTACTICALLYb.', whose length is 41. In order to accommodate *any* string value of length 41 (including this one), the declaration SENT must be written as:

DCL SENT CHAR (41);

On the other hand, to accommodate any string value of length 41 *or less*, the declaration would be rewritten as:

DCL SENT CHAR (41) VAR;

In this second case, the value of SENT may at one time be a string of length 41 and at another time be a string of length 5. Thus, the length, as well as the value, of a string variable can change when its declaration contains the word VARYING.

2-1.2 Arrays

It is often useful in programming to represent, in the form of a tabular list, a collection of values with the same type. For example, we might like to represent a list of the individual words in a sentence. If ordinary variables are used for this purpose, we must invent a distinct name for each word in order to store it separately. The sentence 'EACH PREPOSITION OPERATES SYNTACTI-CALLY .' might be partitioned among the variables WORD1, WORD2, WORD3, and WORD4 as follows:

WORD1 | EACH | WORD2 | PREPOSITION | WORD3 | OPERATES |

WORD4 | SYNTACTICALLY |

We can declare these variables as follows:

```
DCL WORD1 CHAR (30) VAR;
DCL WORD2 CHAR (30) VAR;
DCL WORD3 CHAR (30) VAR;
DCL WORD4 CHAR (30) VAR;
```

A slight economy of expression can be gained from the fact that several variables of the same type can be grouped within a single declaration, as follows:

```
DCL (WORD1, WORD2, WORD3, WORD4) CHAR (30) VAR;
```

However, this does not really address the main problem here, since we used a new variable name for each separate word in the sentence. Typically, a sentence will contain more than four words, and we would have to invent far more than four new variable names.

To remedy this situation, the *array* can be used. An array is an ordered list of values that are all known by the same name. Each value is distinguished from the others by appending a *subscript* to the arrays' name. For example, suppose that we want to identify as an array the individual words in a sentence. We may name the array WORDS, and assume that no sentence will have more than say 100 words and no word will have more than 30 characters. Pictorially, the array WORDS can be drawn as follows:

Each individual entry in an array is identified by a unique subscript, which is an integer enclosed in parentheses and appended to the right of the array name. For instance, if we want to identify the third entry in the array WORDS, we write:

WORDS(3)

More generally, if we want to reference the Ith entry of an array, where I is a variable with some integer value between 1 and 100, we can write:

WORDS(I)

Thus, arrays allow us to assign a generic name to a collection of values, and to identify each value uniquely by using a subscript.
To declare an array, the following kind of declaration can be used:

DCL name (size) type ;

Here, "name" identifies an array, "size" identifies its number of entries, and "type" identifies their type. For instance, the array WORDS described above may be declared as:

DCL WORDS (100) CHAR (30) VAR;

In typical situations, not all of an array is used. We often declare an array so that its size will accommodate the largest number of entires that could practically occur. For example, we have assumed for the array WORDS that the largest sentence will not exceed 100 words. (If this assumption cannot be made, there are several other ways of dealing with the problem of varying sentence length.

Nevertheless, we can declare an array with some extra space, and then require the program to keep a counter that tells exactly how many entries are actually in use. Reconsider the sentence

'EACH PREPOSITION OPERATES SYNTACTICALLY .'

as it would appear in our array WORDS:

```
WORDS                        NWORDS
+---------------+            +-----+
|   EACH        |            |  4  |
+---------------+-+          +-----+
| PREPOSITION     |
+---------------+-+
| OPERATES      |
+---------------+---+
| SYNTACTICALLY     |
+-------------------+
```

Here, the counter NWORDS indicates the number of entries that are in use for this particular sentence.

2-2   Elementary Input and Output

Now that we have variables and arrays for storing data values in memory, we next introduce PL/I facilities which bring values into these locations from an external medium and deliver values from these locations to an external medium. As we recall from Chapter 1, these facilities are known as input and output operations. Input data are usually encoded on some computer-readable medium, such as punched cards, magnetic tape, or magnetic disk.

For the moment, we consider only punched cards as an input medium; tape and disk input will be discussed in Section 2-8. A single punched card can accommodate 80 characters of information. The particular locations on the card that the data occupy, as well as the number of data cards that contain the entire collection of input data, will vary depending upon the data. The programmer is generally free to design the data layout in a variety of ways. Either of the following two conventions can be used to encode a series of sentences on punched cards:

(1) Encode each sentence as a string value, with its enclosing apostrophes (') and followed by at least one blank space.

```
'EACH PREPOSITION OPERATES SYNTACTICALLY.'
```

(2) Encode each sentence as a character string without its enclosing quotes, beginning in column 1 and followed by at least one blank space.

col. 1
↓

```
EACH PREPOSITION OPERATES SYNTACTICALLY .
```

To transfer a data value from an input card to a variable in memory, one of the following forms of the "GET statement" can be used:

(1) GET LIST (name);
(2) GET EDIT (name) (format);

The choice between these two forms is determined by which of the above two data encoding conventions is used. Form 1 of the GET statement is used with the first encoding convention, and form 2 is used with the second.

In either form, "name" denotes the name of the variable where the input data value will be stored. In the second form, 'format' denotes a description of the particular length and starting position (on the input card) of the data value. This is required because of the absence of enclosing apostrophes on the card to delimit the string's beginning and end.

To illustrate, suppose that the variable named SENT is declared as:

```
DCL SENT CHAR (41);
```

The following GET statement transfers the string from the *first* card shown above to the variable named SENT:

```
GET LIST (SENT);
```

Alternatively, the string from the *second* card can be transferred to SENT by way of the following GET statement.

```
GET EDIT (SENT) (COL(1), A(41)) ;
```

Here, the format is "COL(1), A(41)." This means literally that the string to be transferred begins in column 1 of the card and is 41 characters in length. Both statements therefore leave the same value in SENT.

In short, the choice between the two forms of the GET statement is determined by whether or not the data are encoded in a fixed, predetermined format on the input card. If so, the 'format' part of the GET EDIT statement describes exactly where the data are located. If not, data values on the card must be mutually separated by at least one space, and all strings must be enclosed in apostrophes.

For a single GET statement, several values may be transferred from an input card, rather than just one. To accomplish this, a list of variable names is given in the GET statement, and a series of corresponding data values are provided on the input card. When the GET statement is executed, the input data values are transferred to the listed variables in a left-to-right manner. To illustrate, suppose we have the following three data values on a card:

```
 37      'EACH'     70.53
```

Nore here that each value is followed by at least one space. Suppose further that the following three variables have been declared:

```
DCL  I FIXED BIN,
     WORD CHAR (4),
     AMT FIXED DEC (4,2);
```

Then execution of the statement GET LIST (I,WORD,AMT); will leave these variables with the following values:

I | 37 | WORD | EACH | AMT | 70.53 |

Note that the order in which the variables are listed in the GET statement determines the order in which the values themselves are assigned.

Until now, we have been careful to declare variables with types that exactly match the values on the input data card. For example, the variable AMT is declared as FIXED DEC (4,2) and the value 70.53 on the input card matched these specifications exactly. A certain amount of latitude is possible here, since in most practical situations the values of a series of input numbers or character strings will not be identical in type. For instance, a series of words will not all be the same length and a series of numbers will not all be the same scale, as shown in the following two examples:

'EACH' 'PREPOSITION' 'OPERATES' 'SYNTACTICALLY'

37 -1.73 0 0.00025

When declaring a string variable, one must find a length that will accommodate the longest input value. In the case of single words, a maximum length of 30 is practical, e.g.,

DCL WORD CHAR (30) VAR;

When declaring a numeric variable, the same kind of provision should be made; anticipate the largest number that will occur and declare the precision (p,q) appropriately. In the case of the series of numbers shown above, five decimal digits and seven total significant digits will be adequate to accommodate all of them, for example,

DCL NMBR FIXED DEC (7,5);

Since the variable NMBR will hold only a number of the form xx.xxxxx, the numbers shown in the above input card would be stored, respectively, as:

37.00000   -01.73000   00.00000   00.00025

Whenever a string variable is too short to accommodate the length of a string value, the value itself will be truncated on the right end to accommodate the maximum length of the variable. For instance, if we declare

DCL WORD CHAR (4);

and then input the string 'PREPOSITION' then the value of WORD will be

WORD | PREP |

On the other hand, if the variable is too long for the string, extra blanks (b) are appended to the right of the string to "fill out" the variable. For instance, if we input the string 'IN' for the variable WORD as declared above, then the value of WORD will become:

WORD | INbb |

Truncation on the right occurs for decimal numeric values, when the number of decimal digits allowed by q in the variable's declaration is less than that in the value itself. For instance, the value 0.00025 will be stored as

J $\boxed{0.0002}$

when J is declared a FIXED DEC (5,4) and as

J $\boxed{0}$

when J is declared as either FIXED BIN or FIXED DEC (1,0).

However, when the declaration of a numeric variable would cause loss of significant high-order digits for a particular input data value, execution of the GET statement may be interrupted and that value may not be assigned to that variable. For example, if we declare J as FIXED DEC (1,0) and attempt to input the value 25 from a card and store it in J, there is not room in J for the high-order digit 2 and an error will result. Further discussion of this situation and its proper treatment is deferred to Section 2-9.

For output, data are transferred from memory to an output medium, such as printed paper, magnetic tape, magnetic disk, or punched cards. We consider in this section only the printed output of data. Other output media are discussed in Section 2-8.

Output may be printed using either of the following two forms of the PUT statement:

(1) PUT LIST (name or value);
(2) PUT EDIT (name or value) (format);

The first form is used when the data are to be printed in a continuous "stream," with the program having no control over the particular location or representation of the value printed. The second form is used, on the other hand, when such control is to be exercised.

Here, "name or value" means that either a variable's name or a particular (numeric or string) value may be designated for output. "Format" is used to describe the particular location and layout for the value on the printed page. Although not indicated by these two forms of the PUT statement, a list of two or more variable names and/or values may also be given. In that case, the individual values in the list are printed in the order that they are listed.

To illustrate, suppose we have SENT declared as CHAR(16) and NWORDS declared as FIXED BIN with the following values:

SENT | EACH   PREPOSITION |

NWORDS | 2 |

Execution of the PUT statement

```
PUT LIST (SENT);
```

simply causes the value 'EACH PREPOSITION' to be printed in the next available position on the page.

The "next available position" means the following: The printed page is assumed to be divided into 60 lines and 132 characters per line.[2] In the case of the PUT LIST statement, each line is additionally assumed to be divided into six tab positions: 1, 25, 49, 73, 97, and 121. Initially, the first available position is position 1 on the first line of the first page. As each successive PUT statement is executed, the next available position is found by moving to the right from one tab position to the next, and then vertically from one line to the next, as shown in Fig. 2-1. For the PUT LIST statement, the next available position is the next available tab position following the data that has most recently been printed. For the PUT EDIT statement, the next available position is literally the next position following the data that has most recently been printed.

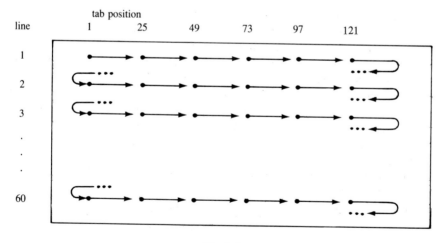

Fig. 2-1

[2] This particular information is installation dependent.

Consider the following illustrations for SENT and NWORDS, as defined above, assuming in each case that the next available position is position 1 of line 1:

PUT Statement	Output
	posn 1
(i) PUT LIST (SENT);	'EACH PREPOSITION'
	1-10
(ii) PUT LIST (NWORDS);	4
	1
(iii) PUT EDIT (SENT) (A(16)0);	EACH PREPOSITION
	1
(iv) PUT EDIT (SENT) (A);	EACH PREPOSITION
	10
(v) PUT EDIT (SENT) (COL(10),A);	EACH PREPOSITION
	1
(vi) PUT EDIT (SENT) (A(4));	EACH
	1
(vii) PUT EDIT (SENT, 'HASb', NWORDS, 'bWORDS.') (A,COL(1),A,F(3),A);	EACH PREPOSITION HAS bb2 WORDS

Most of these examples are self-explanatory. Notice that the A format item can be provided without a length (example iv), in which case the length of the string itself governs the number of characters printed. The COL format specification causes forward skipping to a position on the current line (example v), or the next line in the event that that position has already been passed on the current line (example vii). Example vi shows that truncation of a string can occur in output when the length given by the A format is shorter than that of the string. Example vii also shows how several values can be printed by a single PUT statement, and how a numeric data value is printed using the F format specification.

The various format specifications that can accompany the PUT EDIT statement are described below.

Format specification	Description
A(w)	Print a character string value in the next w positions. If w is less than the string's length, truncation takes place. If w is greater, the string is "padded" on the right with blanks to achieve a length of w.

Format specification	Description
COL(n)	Skip forward to COLumn (position) n of the current line. If it has already been passed, then skip forward to COLumn n of the next line.
F(w) or F(w,d)	Print a numeric value in the next w positions. "d" designates the number of decimal positions. If d is omitted, zero (0) decimal positions are printed.
LINE(n)	Skip forward to position 1 of line n on the current page. If already passed, skip forward to position 1 of line n on the *next* page.
PAGE	Skip forward to position 1 of line 1 on the next page.
SKIP(n)	Skip forward to position 1 of the nth line *beyond* the current line.

These are all self-explanatory, except for the F specification. The following list shows how the value 11.25 is printed under different F specifications:

F specification	Value printed
F(5,2)	11.25
F(4,1)	11.3
F(3,0)	ƀ11
F(3)	ƀ11
F(6,3)	11.250
F(6,2)	ƀ11.25
F(4,2)	*Error;* the difference between w and d is not large enough to print 11.25 without losing high-order significant digits.

Note here that the value given for w must provide positions for the sign and decimal point (if any) as well as each decimal digit in the value itself. Thus, the pair "w,d" is not identical in meaning with the pair (p,q) that appears as the precision of a FIXED DECIMAL variable.

To transfer values into an array from punched cards, or out of an array to printed paper, only the array's name needs to be given in the corresponding GET or PUT statement. For example, suppose we have again the array WORDS, declared as:

```
DCL WORDS(4) CHAR(30) VAR;
```

Given the input data card

```
'EACH'  'PREPOSITION'  'OPERATES'  'SYNTACTICALLY'
```

the statement below will leave WORDS as shown on the right.

GET LIST (WORDS);

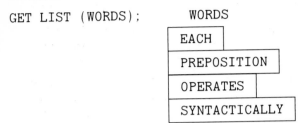

This is therefore an abbreviated equivalent to

GET LIST (WORDS(1), WORDS (2), WORDS(3), WORDS(4));

Similarly, the following PUT statement will leave the values in WORDS printed as shown on the right:

```
                                          col 1
PUT EDIT (WORDS) (4 (COL(1), A));    EACH
                                     PREPOSITION
                                     OPERATES
                                     SYNTACTICALLY
```

Note here the allowable abbreviation that we used instead of saying COL(1), A, COL(1), A, COL(1), A, COL(1), A, which would have been more tedious to write. Note also that when an array is specified in a GET or PUT statement with format specifications, there must be one format item for each element in the array.

2-3 Arithmetic and Assignment

It is often necessary to assign a value to a variable, or else change the value of a variable, *without* performing an input (GET) operation. For instance, if a program is to count the number of words in a sentence, it will need to add 1 to the value of a variable, say NWORDS, each time it identifies the next word in the sentence it is scanning.

The vehicle for assigning, or changing, the value of a variable is the *assignment statement*. Its basic form is

name = expression ;

Here, "name" denotes the name of a variable, and "expression" describes a value that will be assigned to the variable.

In its simplest form, "expression" can be merely a value—numeric or string—to be assigned to the variable named on the left. For instance, if we write the assignment statement

```
NWORDS = 0 ;
```

we are assigning the numeric value 0 to the numeric variable NWORDS, with the following result:

NWORDS | 0 |

Similarly, if we write the assignment statement

```
SENT = 'EACH PREPOSITION OPERATES SYNTACTICALLY .';
```

we are assigning a string value to the string variable SENT, as follows:

SENT | EACH PREPOSITION OPERATES SYNTACTICALLY . |

In general, the type—numeric or string—of the expression on the right side of the assignment statement should agree with that of the variable on the left.

More elaborate forms of expressions exist both for describing numeric values and for describing string values. In the case of numbers, an expression may describe a series of one or more arithmetic operations which, when performed, will deliver a single numeric result. Each arithmetic operation has two operands, which may be either variables or numeric constants. The arithmetic operations are as follows:

Arithmetic operation	Meaning
+	Addition
−	Subtraction
*	Multiplication
/	Division
**	Exponentiation

Thus, for example, if we write the expression

```
NWORDS + 1
```

we are designating the sum of the current value of NWORDS and 1. Furthermore, if we put this on the right side of an assignment statement,

```
NWORDS = NWORDS +1;
```

we are saying "add 1 to the value of NWORDS and then assign the result as the new value of NWORDS." Whenever an expression appears on the right side of an assignment statement, it is evaluated *first*, and the resulting value is then assigned to the variable on the left.

Expressions can contain more than one arithmetic operator. For instance, we can compute the average number of words (AVWORDS) between two sentences, knowing that the number of words in each is NWORDS1 and NWORDS2, by the following algebraic calculations:

$$\text{AVWORDS} = \frac{\text{NWORDS1} + \text{NWORDS2}}{2}$$

Unfortunately, PL/I does not permit an expression to be written on more than one line; it must be "linearized", with the aid of parentheses, as follows:

```
AVWORDS  =  (NWORDS1+NWORDS2)/2;
```

Note here that we are acknowledging the usual precedence of division over addition (as in algebra) by using parentheses to designate that the addition be performed before the division.

Generally, addition and subtraction have lower precedence than multiplication and division, and these in turn yield precedence to exponentiation. Parentheses must be used whenever the order of evaluation implied by that precedence is not desired, as in the previous example.

Finally, when two or more operators of the same precedence appear at the same level of parenthesization in an expression, they are performed from left to right. The following example illustrates these points:

```
A  =  B+C*(D+E-F);
      ④ ③  ① ②
```

Here, the numbered arrows indicate the sequence in which the four operations in the expression are performed.

We defer discussion of string expressions and assignments until Sections 2-5 and 2-6. There they are given extensive treatment, and several examples are presented.

2-3.1 Array Assignment

Before leaving this section, we briefly illustrate a very useful assignment facility for arrays. All the elements of an array may be assigned a particular value by the way of the assignment statement

```
array name  =  expression ;
```

where "array name" is the name of the entire array. For instance, if we have the array WORDS declared as

```
DCL WORDS(4) CHAR(30) VAR;
```

then the following assignment statement will leave all four entries in WORDS with the value 'EACH', as shown on the right:

```
WORDS = 'EACH';
```

WORDS

EACH
EACH
EACH
EACH

On the other hand, if we wanted to assign the value 'EACH' to only the first entry in WORDS, we would have given

```
WORDS(1) = 'EACH';
```

Perhaps the most useful purpose of the array assignment statement is to initialize an array of strings to null (''), or an array of number to zero (0). For example, this is achieved for the array WORDS as

```
WORDS = '';
```

2-3.2 Initialization of Variables and Arrays in the Declaration

The same effect as the assignment statement can be achieved by using the so-called INITIAL attribute in the declaration of a variable or array when it is desired to assign initial constant value(s) to it. If we want, for example, to set the value of NWORDS to zero (0) initially, we can write

```
DCL NWORDS FIXED BIN INIT (0);
```

To initialize the array WORDS to null, we can write

```
DCL WORDS(4) CHAR(30) VAR INIT ((4)'');
```

Here, we have assigned the null string value to each of the four entries in the array WORDS. Note also that the INITIAL attribute contains a description of four string values (rather than one, as in the previous assignment statement), and that the notation

```
(4) ''
```

is just an abbreviation for writing:

```
'','','',''
```

If we had written, on the other hand, only one string value for this initialization, only the first entry in WORDS, WORDS(1), would have been assigned an initial value.

The requirement to list all the initial values for an array's entries within an INITIAL attribute can sometimes be an advantage, since it allows different values to be assigned to different entries. For example, we can assign four different values to the WORDS array as follows:

```
DCL WORDS(4) CHAR(30) VAR INIT ('EACH', 'PREPOSITION',
'OPERATES', 'SYNTACTICALLY');
```

(Note here that we have broken the declaration into two separate lines. This is generally permitted for *any* PL/I statement.) Whenever all the values to be assigned are different, we must list them in the order in which they should be assigned to the different entries. In this example, 'EACH' will become the value of WORDS(1), 'PREPOSITION' of WORDS(2), and so forth.

2-4 Complete Programs and Control Statements

Every PL/I program must begin with a "PROCEDURE statement" and end with an "END statement." The PROCEDURE statement can be written as

```
name: PROCEDURE OPTIONS (MAIN);
```

The END statement has the form

```
  END name;
```

In each instance, "name" denotes the name of the program, and must be composed of 7 or fewer letters[3] and/or digits, the first being a letter. Furthermore, the appearance of "name" in the END statement can optionally be omitted. Between these two statements are all the declarations and statements that describe the functioning of the program. Here, for example, is a complete PL/I program named PGM1, which reads and prints the contents of a single 80-column input data card:

```
PGM1: PROC OPTIONS (MAIN);
    DCL CARD CHAR (80);
    GET EDIT (CARD) (A(80));
    PUT EDIT (CARD) (COL(1), A(80));
    END PGM1;
```

[3] This is installation dependent.

The individual words within each PL/I statement must be separated by one or more blank spaces, unless some delimiter (such as $+$, $-$, (,), :, and so forth) occurs between them. In the above program, for instance, one or more spaces must separate PROC and OPTIONS, but not OPTIONS and MAIN since (occurs between them.

More often than not, we need the ability to change the order of statement execution from the textual order in which the statements appear. For example, in order to read and print an entire deck of input data cards, the example program PGM1 would have to be modified so that the GET and PUT statements would be executed several times.

To modify the sequence of program execution, PL/I has different kinds of "control statements":

(1)   the IF statement,
(2)   the DO statement,
(3)   the GO TO statement,
(4)   the CALL statement,
(5)   the ON statement.

We discuss each of these individually in the following paragraphs.

2-4.1   The IF Statement

The IF statement is used to specify that some other statement or sequence of statements should be executed whenever a particular condition is true. The IF statement can be written in either of two ways:

(1)   IF condition THEN statement1
(2)   IF condition THEN statement1 ELSE statement2

Here, "condition" denotes a relational expression that must be true in order for "statement1" to be executed. Otherwise, "statement1" will be skipped. When form 2 of the IF statement is used, "statement2" will be executed exactly when "condition" is not true.

Before describing how conditions are written, let us consider a practical situation that requires the IF statement. Suppose that we have an array named WORDS of 100 words and we want to keep a count of the number of occurrences of the article THE among them. Suppose further that this count is kept by the variable N, and that the variable I is used as a subscript for the array WORDS. Then the following IF statement will cause N to be incremented only if the Ith entry in WORDS is 'THE':

```
IF  WORD(I)  =  'THE'  THEN  N=N+1;
```

We shall complete this problem after presenting the DO statement below.

A "condition" may be either a relation or a logical combination of relations. A relation is formed by giving one of the following relational operators between two operands, which may in turn be any arithmetic or string expressions.

Relational operator (op)	Meaning of "*a* op *b*"
<	*a* is less then *b*
=	*a* and *b* are equal
>	*b* is less than *a*
<=	*a* is less than or equal to *b*
>=	*b* is less than or equal to *a*
¬ =	*a* and *b* are not equal

When the operands *a* and *b* are arithmetic expressions, these relations reflect the usual ordering among numbers. When *a* and *b* are string expressions, these relations denote alphabetical, or "dictionary" ordering among strings. In this case, it is assumed that the following order exists among the single characters:

$$\text{'}ƀ\text{'} < \{\text{all special characters}\} < \text{'A'} < \text{'B'} < \cdots < \text{'Z'} < \text{'0'} < \text{'1'} < \cdots < \text{'9'}$$

A string *a* is said to be "less than" a string *b* if one of the following is true:

(1) *a* and *b* are of the same length n and there is an integer k with $0 \le k < n$, such that the first k characters of *a* are respectively identical with the first k character of *b* and the (k + 1)th character of *a* is less than the (k + 1)th character of *b* (according to the ordering given above).

(2) *a* and *b* are of unequal length, but the addition of enough blanks at the right hand end of the shorter one to equalize their lengths causes satisfaction of 1 above.

Two strings, *a* and *b*, are equal (i.e., "*a* = *b*" is true) if either

(1) they are the same length and they are identical, character for character;
or
(2) they are of unequal length, but the addition of enough blanks at the right-hand end of the shorter one to equalize their lengths makes them identical, character for character.

Two relations within IF statements illustrate some of these points:

```
IF I <= 10 THEN I=I+1;
```
                                            Here I will be
                                            incremented only
                                            if its value is not
                                            greater than 10.

```
IF  WORD(I) = '␢'  THEN  WORD(I) = 'THE';
```
Here, the Ith entry of WORD will be left as 'THE', but only if it is currently blank.

Conditions can also be formed from other conditions by use of the logical conjunction and disjunction operators & and |, respectively. If r and s are relations, then "r & s" is true only if both r and s are true. For example, the following IF statement will leave the value of WORD(I) as 'THE' only if both I $<=$ 10 and WORD(I) $=$ '␢' are true:

```
IF I <= 10 & WORD(I) = '␢' THEN WORD(I) = 'The';
```

Any number of such relations may be combined using the & and the | operators. If both appear within the same condition, & takes precedence over |. That precedence may be overridden by parentheses, just as it is among arithmetic operators.

2-4.2   The DO Statement

Many programming situations arise where a group of statements, rather than a single statement, are treated logically as an indivisible entity. For example, suppose we are interested in counting the number of occurrences N of the article 'THE' in the array WORDS, as introduced in the foregoing section. To accomplish this task may, indeed, require several statements.

The DO statement is one device for grouping several statements together. It is used when the statement group is to be executed in either of the following ways.

(1)   The statements in the group are to be executed once, but only if a particular condition is true.

(2)   The statements in the group are to be executed repeatedly, either a countable number of times or until a particular condition becomes false.

The following two forms of the DO statement accommodate these two situations respectively:

(1)   IF condition THEN DO;
$$\boxed{\text{sequence of statements}}$$
      END;

(2)   DO variable = e_1 TO e_2 WHILE (condition);
$$\boxed{\text{sequence of statements}}$$
      END;

In both cases, the enclosed "sequence of statements" may contain any number of statements: I/O statements, assignment statements, and so forth. In the first case, that sequence will be executed only if "condition" is true. In the second case, e_1 and e_2 denote expressions that will be evaluated upon execution of the DO statement. Execution of the sequence of statements will be repeated at most $e_2 - e_1 + 1$ times, but may be terminated immediately before any repetition if the designated "condition" is false. That is, the condition is tested immediately before each repetition, including the first. Finally, the "variable" will have its value set initially to the value of e_1 and incremented by 1 immediately before each repetition of the sequence of statements. Repetition of a sequence of statements in this way is often called a "loop" and the variable is often called the loop's "control variable."

To illustrate, recall the problem of counting the number of occurrences of the article 'THE' in the 100-entry array named WORDS. We assume here that WORDS does not necessarily contain 100 words, but its last word is followed immediately by a null string.

```
N = 0;
DO I = 1 TO 100 WHILE (WORDS(I) ¬= ");
        IF WORDS(I) = 'THE' THEN N = N+1;
        END;
```

Here, the sequence of statements will be repeated at most 100 times, and will be terminated early if the condition WORDS(I) ¬= " becomes false. The sequence itself contains only one statement, the IF statement, which increments N each time 'THE' is detected. The control variable I takes on successive integer values beginning with 1 and thus also serves as the subscript for referencing successive entries in the array WORDS.

Before concluding our discussion of DO statements we must mention the following useful alternative forms of DO statements:

(3)   IF condition
      THEN DO;

      | sequence of statements |

              END;
      ELSE DO;

      | sequence of statements |

              END;
(4)   DO variable = e_1 TO e_2;

      | sequence of statements |

              END;

(5) DO variable $= e_1$ TO e_2 BY e_3;

> | sequence of statements |

   END;

Form 3 is a logical extension of form 1, using the ELSE option of the IF statement. The sequence that follows ELSE will be executed exactly when "condition" is false. Form 4 represents that special case of form 2 where the sequence is to be executed *exactly* $e_2 - e_1 + 1$ times, without being prematurely terminated. Form 5 shows how a loop's control variable can be changed by some value other than $+1$ after each repetition of the sequence. For example,

```
DO I = I TO 100 BY 2;
```

specifies for I the succession of values 1,3,5, ... The statement

```
DO I = 100 TO 1 BY −1;
```

on the other hand, specifies for I the succession of values 100, 99, 98, ...
   Finally, the value of a loop's control variable, upon exit from the sequence of statements, is defined for form 2 as follows. Before each execution of the sequence of statements, the following condition is tested:

variable $\leq e_2$

If this is true, then the sequence is executed. Otherwise, repetition ceases and the next statement following the loop is executed. After each execution of the sequence, the control variable is incremented by $+1$, and the condition is tested again. Thus, when repetition ceases, the control variable's value is greater than the limit e_2. Note also that it is possible for the sequence to be executed zero times.
   The meaning of form 5 is similarly defined, except that whenever the increment value e_3 is negative (i.e., is a decrement) the condition that is tested for continuance of the loop becomes

variable $\geq e_2$

Here, exit from the loop leaves the control variable less than the limit e_2. Thus, the two DO statements

```
DO I = 1 to 100 BY 2;
DO I = 100 TO 1 BY −1;
```

leave the final value of I at 101 and 0, respectively. We shall have further use for all these forms of the DO statement in later sections.

2-4.3 The GO TO Statement

Any statement in the program may be prefixed optionally by a *label*, which serves to uniquely identify the statement. The label can be any sequence of letters and digits, the first being a letter, which is followed by a colon (:). For instance, the statement

```
IF WORDS(I)  =  'THE'  THEN N  =  N+1;
```

may be prefixed with the label COUNTIT as follows:

```
COUNTIT:  IF WORDS(I)  =  'THE'  THEN N  =  N+1;
```

The utility of labeling a statement arises when we need to transfer control to it from the current point of execution. The GO TO *statement* is used for this, and its form is

```
GO TO label;
```

Here, "label" designates the label of the statement where control should be transferred. For example, consider the following sequence of statements:

```
          N = 0;
          I = 1;
LOOP:     IF I <= 100
          THEN IF WORDS(I)⌐ = '' THEN GO TO COUNTIT;
             ELSE GO TO EXIT;
          ELSE GO TO EXIT;
COUNTIT:  IF WORDS(I)  =  'THE'  THEN N  =  N+1;
          I = I+1;
          GO TO LOOP:
EXIT:
```

Here, there are several GO TO statements. A careful reading should reveal that these statements are logically equivalent to the previous DO loop, which counted the number of occurrences of 'THE' in the array WORDS.

In general, the number of GO TO statements and labels in a program should be minimized. Program logic tends to be difficult to read when the program text is cluttered with unnecessary labels and GO TO statements. For instance, the following illustrates how some judicious reprogramming can claify the statements shown above:

```
          N = 0;
          I = 1;
LOOP:     IF I <= 100
          THEN IF WORDS(I)= ''
                THEN DO;
```

```
IF WORDS(I)  =  'THE'  THEN  N  =  N+1;
I  =  I+1;
GO TO LOOP;
END;
```

Here, we have eliminated all but one GO TO statement and all but one label. In the process, the programming logic has become more visible. Of course, this version is still inferior to the original version, which used the repetitive DO statement in place of the statements that set, increment, and test the control variable I

2-4.4   The CALL Statement

As the size and complexity of a programming task grows, so does the program and the need to keep its logic readable. Several points for good programming style have already been made. However, the most important program organization tool is found in the CALL *statement* and the associated *subprogram* concept.

Like the DO statement, the CALL statement causes execution of a sequence of statements and allows that sequence to be treated logically as an indivisible entity. Unlike the DO statement, however, the CALL statement allows that sequence to be textually removed, or isolated, from the CALL statement itself. This is an entirely new level of programming flexibility, since the same sequence of statements can be CALLed, or executed, from several different logical locations within the program, and without being rewritten each time it is executed.

When CALLed in this way, the sequence of statements is identified within the program as a *procedure* in the following manner:

name: PROCEDURE;

> sequence of statements

    END name;

Here, "name" identifies the procedure, and has the same formation rules as the name of the program itself.

However, the presence of a procedure within a program serves only to *define* a task. *Execution* of that task does not occur until a CALL statement within the main program is reached. The basic form of the CALL statement is

CALL name;

Here, "name" denotes the name of the procedure whose task is to be executed. When execution of the procedure's statements is completed, the statement following the CALL is next executed. Execution of the main program then continues until the next CALL statement is encountered.

To illustrate, suppose we wish to write a procedure within a main program, which counts the number of occurrences of the article 'THE' in the array WORDS, as described in previous sections. We shall name this procedure COUNTER, in accordance with its purpose, and define it as

```
COUNTER:  PROC;
          N = 0;
          DO I = 1 TO 100;
            IF WORDS(I) = 'THE' THEN N = N+1;
            END;
          END COUNTER;
```

Once defined, this procedure may be embedded within any program that requires its particular task. That task may be actually executed by writing

```
CALL COUNTER;
```

at the particular logical point within the program where this task is needed.

To demonstrate the use of procedures for subdividing a larger programming task into smaller ones, suppose we want to write a program that performs the following series of tasks for each one of an arbitrary number of sentences:

Task	Name
(1) Read a particular sentence and store in the varying length character string variable named SENT.	READER
(2) Break the sentence into its individual words and store them in the array WORDS.	BREAKER
(3) Count the number of occurrences of 'THE' in the array WORDS.	COUNTER
(4) Print the sentence, SENT, and the number N of articles 'THE'.	PRINTER

We shall assume that these four functions are performed by the four procedures whose names are listed in the right-hand column above. Furthermore, we shall assume that the string variable SENT, the array WORDS, and the counters NW and N serve the purposes described in the following declaration:

```
DCL SENT CHAR(500) VAR INIT ("),
          /* CONTAINS A SINGLE SENTENCE
          AND WILL BE INITIALIZED BY THE PROCEDURE
          'READER' */
```

```
WORDS (100)CHAR(30) VAR INIT ((100) "),
            /* CONTAINS THE INDIVIDUAL WORDS OF THE
            SENTENCE IN SENT, AND WILL BE ESTABLISHED
            BY THE PROCEDURE 'BREAKER' */
   NW FIXED BIN, /* COUNTS THE NUMBER OF WORDS IN
            SENT, AND WILL ALSO BE ESTABLISHED BY
            THE PROCEDURE 'BREAKER' */
   N FIXED BIN; /* COUNTS THE NUMBER OF ARTICLES
            'THE' IN WORDS, AND WILL BE ESTABLISHED
            BY THE PROCEDURE 'COUNTER' */
```

We have already written the procedure COUNTER. The procedures READER and PRINTER can be written simply, and in any of a number of ways, depending on the format of the input and output. The procedure BREAKER can be written after we have presented some string processing functions in Section 2-6. Here we focus attention on the main program. It must invoke these procedures in the proper sequence, in order to accomplish its general task. The entire program, including its four embedded procedures, has the following overall structure:

```
PGM2: PROCEDURE OPTIONS (MAIN);
        DCL SENT CHAR (500) VAR Init ').
            WORDS (100) CHAR (30) VAR INIT ((100) ");
            NW FIXED BIN,
            N FIXED BIN;
        READER: PROC;
            ⋮
            END READER;
        BREAKER; PROC;
            ⋮
            END BREAKER;
        COUNTER: PROC;
            ⋮
            END COUNTER;
        PRINTER: PROC;
            ⋮
            END PRINTER;
/* BELOW IS THE MAIN LOGIC THAT CONTROLS EXECUTION OF THIS
PROGRAM */
DO WHILE ('1'B);
    CALL READER;        /* READ A SENTENCE */
```

```
    CALL BREAKER;       /* BREAK IT INTO WORDS */
    CALL COUNTER;       /* COUNT N = NO. OF 'THE's */
    CALL PRINTER;       /* PRINT THE SENTENCE AND N */
    END;
END PGM2;
```

The principal value of organizing programs in this way lies in the readability and separability of tasks that it permits. Subsequent program modifications tend to be easily localized. For instance, we can alter the format of input data representation by changing only the READER procedure; the rest of the program remains unchanged.

There are a couple of "loose ends" in this program that we have not yet fully explained. First, notice that we have used the following form of the DO statement:

```
DO WHILE ('1'B);
```

The '1'B here is a *bit string,* which represents the logical value "true," while '0'B represents the logical value "false." Thus, this DO statement specifies indefinite repetition of its sequence of statements, since true is always true.

This leads to the second loose end in our program: when and how will the program stop executing? It will stop after it has processed all of the sentences in the input data. Since we have not specified what to do when this event actually occurs, an error message will be printed. That message will indicate that the program tried to read input data when, in fact, no more input data remained to be read. The program will be executing a GET statement within the READER procedure when this event actually occurs.

2-4.5 The ON Statement

The last program control statement that we discuss in this section is the ON statement. It is used when some unusual condition arises during program execution. There are several such unusual conditions defined within the PL/I language. One of these is discussed in the previous paragraph: an attempt to read input data when, in fact, no more remain to be read. This event is known in PL/I as ENDFILE(SYSIN). The condition is said to be *raised* when the event actually occurs during program execution.

For the program to take a specific action when a condition is raised, it must contain an ON statement. The ON statement can be written in either of the following two ways:

(1)   ON condition statement
(2)   ON condition BEGIN;

┌─────────────────────────┐
│ sequence of statements │
└─────────────────────────┘

        END;

The first form is used when the action to be taken can be described in a single statement. Otherwise, the second form is used. In either case, the ON statement must occur textually *ahead* of the first statement in the program where the designated condition can actually be raised. For instance, if we write an ON statement for the condition ENDFILE(SYSIN), it should be placed in the program textually before the first GET statement.

In many cases, the only action that should occur when ENDFILE(SYSIN) is raised is that program execution should stop. The so-called STOP statement, written as

```
STOP;
```

can be placed anywhere in a program to designate stoppage of execution. When it occurs within an ON statement in the following way,

```
ON ENDFILE(SYSIN) STOP;
```

the effect is simply to stop execution when no more input data remain to be read.

In other cases, an entire *series* of actions may be required when the end of input data occurs. For example, a program may be asked to count the total number of occurrences N of the article 'THE' among a series of sentences, examining the sentences one at a time. The value of N in this case cannot be printed until after the end of input data has occurred. In this situation, the following ON statement is suitable.

```
ON ENDFILE(SYSIN) BEGIN;
    PUT EDIT (N,' OCCURRENCES OF "THE" ')
            (F(5),A);
    STOP;
    END;
```

Another use of the ON statement occurs in conjunction with printed output. The condition is known as ENDPAGE(SYSPRINT). It is raised whenever execution of a PUT statement causes skipping beyond the last line of the printed page.

In the absence of an ON statement, any PUT statement that would cause printing beyond the last line of a page is interrupted and the printer automatically advances to the first line of the next page before that PUT statement resumes execution. In many cases, this procedure is perfectly acceptable; output continues from one page to the next, and a small margin is left at the bottom and top of each page.

In other cases, however, this procedure is not acceptable. For example, we might wish to number the output pages or print a heading at the top of each page. We can do this by writing an ON statement for the condition END–

`PAGE(SYSPRINT)`. Whenever that condition is raised, i.e., whenever the bottom of a page is reached, the `ON` statement can be written to put a title at the top of the next page before execution of the `PUT` statement resumes. Consider the following example program:

```
PGM3: PROC OPTION (MAIN);
          DCL PNO FIXED BIN INIT(0),CARD CHAR (80);
          ON ENDFILE(SYSIN) STOP;
          ON ENDPAGE(SYSPRINT) BEGIN;
              PNO = PNO+1;
              PUT EDIT ('CARD LISTING', 'PAGE',
                  PNO) (PAGE,A,COL(90),A,F(4));
              PUT SKIP(2);
              END;
          DO WHILE ('1'B);
              GET EDIT (CARD) (A(80));
              PUT EDIT (CARD) (COL(1),A);
              END;
          END PGM3;
```

This program lists any deck of cards, numbering pages and printing the general, whenever an `ON` statement contains no `GO TO` statement, control is `PAGE(SYSPRINT)` condition is raised by the `PUT` statement, its `ON` statement is executed, causing the heading and a double space to occur on the next page. At that point, control returns to the `PUT` statement where the condition was actually raised, and the line that would have been printed beyond the last line of the previous page is now printed after the heading on the next page. In general whenever an `ON` statement contains no `GO TO` statement, control is said to *normally return* to that point in the program where the condition was actually raised.

2-5   Character String Manipulation: Concatenation, Substrings, and Assignment

At the heart of text processing applications are their string manipulation algorithms. PL/I provides several facilities for manipulating strings. We examine them in this section and the next.

Any string manipulation algorithm can be broken down into a series of relatively primitive operations. One such operation is the joining of two strings end to end to form a single string. For instance, if we join the string `'EA'` and the string `'CH'`, we can form either the string `'EACH'` or the string `'CHEA'`. This joining operation is known as *concatenation*, and PL/I provides the concatenation operator (‖) to specify it. For instance, the concatenation

'EA' ‖ 'CH'

forms the new string 'EACH', while the concatenation

'CH' ‖ 'EA'

forms the new string 'CHEA'.

As a converse to the concatenation operation, another primitive operation separates from a string its constituent substrings. A *substring* of a given string, say s, is any contiguous sequence of zero or more characters in s, including s itself. For example, if 'EACH' is a string, the following are all of its substrings:

' '	'EA'
'E'	'AC'
'A'	'CH'
'C'	'EAC'
'H'	'ACH'
	'EACH'

In PL/I a substring is specified for a given string s by giving its beginning position p in s and its length n. The specification is written as

SUBSTR(s,p,n)

For example, if s is the string 'EACH', then the following shows the effect of some possible substrings specifications:

Substring specification	Effect
SUBSTR('EACH',1,1)	'E'
SUBSTR('EACH',2,3)	'ACH'
SUBSTR('EACH',1,0)	''
SUBSTR('EACH',1,4)	'EACH'
SUBSTR('EACH',5,1) SUBSTR('EACH',2,4)	*Error:* neither of these defines a proper substring of 'EACH'. This causes the STRINGRANGE condition to be raised.

The last two examples in the list are improper substring specifications; in the first case position 5 does not exist in the string 'EACH', and in the second case the longest substring in 'EACH' that begins in position 2 has length 3. Both of these will cause the STRINGRANGE condition to be raised. Like the other conditions, an ON statement can be written for this condition if the program wants to trap it. Otherwise, raising of the STRG condition causes an error message to be printed and program execution to stop.

In general, the arguments s, p, and n within SUBSTR(s,p,n) need not be constants; s can be any string variable or expression, and p and n can be any integer variables or expressions. Richer illustrations of these options occur in later examples. We also note that the abbreviation

SUBSTR(s,p)

can be written to denote that substring of s beginning in position p and continuing to the *end* of s. For instance, SUBSTR('EACH',2) denotes the substring 'ACH'.

The third elementary operation for strings in addition to concatenation and substrings is the assignment of a string value to a string variable. The PL/I assignment statement is used for this. For example, if we declare

```
DCL SENT CHAR (300) VAR,
    WORD CHAR (30) VAR;
```

then the assignment statement

```
SENT = 'EACH PREPOSITION OPERATES SYNTACTICALLY .';
```

leaves SENT with the string value on the right.

Assuming SENT now has that value, we may proceed to concatenate other strings to it, extract substrings from it, or change it altogether by use of concatenation, substring, and assignment operations.

For example, we may extract the first word from SENT and assign it to WORD by the following:

```
WORD = SUBSTR(SENT,1,4);
```

The second word can be stored in WORD as

```
WORD = SUBSTR(SENT,6,11);
```

The reader should note that these are artificial examples, since in general the position and length of a word in an arbitrary sentence are not known by the program in advance (and thus cannot be a fixed constant). We deal more thoroughly with the problem of recognizing words in the next section.

To delete the first word in SENT, i.e., to replace it with blanks, the substring operator can be placed on the left of the assignment statement:

```
SUBSTR(SENT,1,4) = 'bbbb';
```

This will leave the value of SENT as

SENT	bbbbbPREPOSITIONbOPERATESbSYNTACTICALLYb .

Often the length of the string on the right of the assignment differs from the length of the string variable or substring specified on the left. In this case, the length of the string is either extended on the right with blanks or truncated at the right so that its length is equal to that of the variable or substring on the left. However, if the variable is VARYING and the length of the string on the right of the assignment is less than its maximum length, *no* such extension of the right-hand string takes place. The length, as well as the value, of a VARYING variable is changed upon assignment. The following examples illustrate these points, assuming that STR is a CHAR(4) string variable, VSTR is a VARYING CHAR(4) variable, and the assignments are executed in the order shown:

	Resulting value	
Assignment	STR	VSTR
STR = 'ABC';	'ABCƀ'	
VSTR = 'ABC';		'ABC'
STR = 'ABCDE';	'ABCD'	
VSTR = 'ABCDE';		'ABCD'
SUBSTR(STR,2,2) = 'ƀ';	'AƀƀD'	
SUBSTR(VSTR,2,2) = 'ƀ';		'AƀƀD'
STR = SUBSTR(STR,2,1) ‖ 'C';	'ƀCƀƀ'	
VSTR = SUBSTR(VSTR,2,1) ‖ 'C';		'ƀC'

Note that the length of a string variable, whether or not it is VARYING, is *not* affected when a substring of it is specified on the left of an assignment statement. The last two examples show how the concatenation and substring operations can be combined to form the string to be assigned to the variable on the left.

2-6   Built-In Functions for String Manipulation

The main power of PL/I for string manipulation comes from its built-in functions. The substring operation SUBSTR presented above is one such function. Others are INDEX, VERIFY, LENGTH, and TRANSLATE. These are defined in the following table, where s, t, and u denote arbitrary strings, string variables, or string-valued expressions, and i and j denote arbitrary integers, interger variables or integer-valued expressions.

Built-in function	Meaning (result delivered)
INDEX(s,t)	The position of the first character in the leftmost occurrence of t as a substring of s. If t does not occur as a substring of s, the result delivered by INDEX(s,t) is 0.
VERIFY(s,t)	The position of the leftmost character of s which is not in t. If all characters of s are also in t, the result delivered by VERIFY(s,t) is 0.
LENGTH(s)	The number of characters in s, including blanks.

TRANSLATE(s,t,u)   Here, t and u must be strings of the same length.
                        Every character of s that occurs in u is replaced
                        by the character that occurs in the same position
                        in t. Every other character in s is unchanged.

The following examples illustrate the effect of these functions:

Example	Result delivered
INDEX('EACHbPREPOSITION', 'PRE')	6
INDEX('EACHbPREPOSITION', 'THE')	0
VERIFY('EACH', 'AEIOU')	3
VERIFY('EACH', 'ABCDEFGHIJKLMNOPQRSTUVWXYZ')	0
LENGTH('EACH')	4
TRANSLATE('EACH', 'ABCDE', 'EDCBA')	'AECH'

Note that in the last example the character C is actually translated, like A and
E, but its corresponding character in 'ABCDE' is C itself. H, on the other
hand, is not translated.

The principal uses of these functions in text processing are illustrated in the
following examples. Here, we use them as an aid in dissecting a sentence into
its constitutent words. Assume, as before, that we have the following variables
declared:

```
DCL SENT CHAR(300) VAR INIT(
    'EACHbPREPOSITIONbOPERATESbSYNTACTICALLYb.'),
    WORDS(100) CHAR(30) VAR,
    N FIXED BIN INIT (0),
    (I,J) FIXED BIN;
```

We use I and J as auxiliary indices as we pass through the individual words
in SENT; N will be left at the end with the number of words in SENT.

Before solving the problem, observe that the following useful functions are
available:

J = INDEX(SENT,'b');   Gives the location of the
                                leftmost blank in SENT.
                                For the string shown
                                above, this will leave J =
                                5.

I = 6;

```
J = INDEX(SUBSTR(SENT,I),'ƀ');
```
Gives the location of the leftmost blank in the substring of SENT that extends from position 6 to the end. For the string shown above, this will leave J = 12.

In both of these examples, the reader should see that J has been used to identify the *length* of a word in SENT. In the first case, it was assumed that the word begins in position 1 of SENT, and in the second case the word begins in position I.

The only remaining task in the identification of words in a text is to locate the *beginning* of an arbitrary word in SENT:

```
I = VERIFY(SENT,'ƀ');
```
Gives the location of the leftmost nonblank character in SENT. For the string shown above, this will leave I = 1.

```
I = 1; J = 4;
I = VERIFY(SUBSTR(SENT,I+J),
    'ƀ')+I+J−1;
```
Gives the location of the leftmost nonblank character in SENT following the word that begins in position I (= 1) and has length J (= 4).

Thus, if we know the beginning position and length of any word in SENT, we can determine the same for the next word. This process can be described in a loop so that it will continue until the sentence has been exhausted. Furthermore, the isolation of any particular word in SENT can be accomplished by two statements that store it in the next available entry of the array WORDS and increment the counter N. All of this is done in the following loop:

```
I = 1; J = 0;
DO K = 1 TO 100 WHILE (SUBSTR(SENT,I+J) ¬= " ");
    I = VERIFY (SUBSTR(SENT, I + J),'ƀ')+I+J−1;
    J = INDEX(SUBSTR(SENT, I),'ƀ')−1;
        IF J < 0 THEN J = LENGTH(SENT)−I+1;
        WORDS(K) = SUBSTR(SENT,I,J);
        END;
IF K > 100 THEN N = 100; ELSE N = K;
```

To illustrate the effect of this loop, we show how I and J are located immediately before each repetition K for the example sentence given above.

K	I	J	

```
              EACH PREPOSITION OPERATES SYNTACTICALLY .
                ↑
1     1   0   I


              EACH PREPOSITION OPERATES SYNTACTICALLY .
                ↑   ↑
2     1   4   I   J


              EACH PREPOSITION OPERATES SYNTACTICALLY .
                      ↑            ↑
3     6   11        I            J


              EACH PREPOSITION OPERATES SYNTACTICALLY .
                                ↑        ↑
4     18  8                   I        J


              EACH PREPOSITION OPERATES SYNTACTICALLY .
                                        ↑                ↑
5     27  13                          I                J


              EACH PREPOSITION OPERATES SYNTACTICALLY .
                                                          ↑
6     41  1                                              IJ
```

During each of the first five repetitions of the loop, the Kth entry of WORDS is assigned the Kth word in SENT, including the final period. The sixth repetition is actually never executed, since the condition

SUBSTR(SENT,I+J)¬ = "

is no longer true. In that case, the sentence has become exhausted.

Note finally that the last statement is included to ensure that N will not exceed 100. (A sentence with over 100 words will have only its first 100 words actually stored by this algorithm, and K will be left at 101. Here we have made a practical compromise.)

2-7   Extending the Built-In Functions

A number of important string manipulation functions, in addition to those which recognize words, are needed for text processing applications. In this section we develop a collection of additional functions that will enable us to solve a variety of text processing problems.

First, we extend the notions of procedure and CALL statement that were introduced in Section 2-4. When defining a procedure, one may also define one or more *parameters* for it. This is done in the PROCEDURE statement as follows:

name: PROC $(p_1, p_2, \ldots)$;

Here, p_1, p_2, . . . denotes a list of the parameter names.

Associated with each parameter are attributes that denote the kind of data that it represents. This association is given by a declaration within the procedure itself. A varying-length character string parameter is declared as

DCL p_i CHAR $(*)$ VAR;

A fixed binary parameter is declared as

DCL p_i FIXED BIN;

2-7.1   Substring Insertion

Although parameters are not variables, they are treated as though they were variables throughout the body of the procedure. To illustrate, the following procedure will insert any string B between the Ith and $(I + 1)$th characters of the string A:

```
INSERT:  PROC(A,B,I);
         DCL (A,B) CHAR(*) VAR, I FIXED BIN;
         IF I >= 0 & I < LENGTH(A)
         THEN A = SUBSTR(A,1,I) ‖ B ‖ SUBSTR(A,I+1);
         END INSERT;
```

Note that the insertion takes place only if I designates an actual position (from 0 to the length of A minus 1) within A. The 0th position allows insertion at the beginning of A, but no insertion takes place when I ≥ length (A).

To use this procedure and actually perform an insertion, a CALL statement is written that contains a corresponding *argument* for each of the procedure's parameters. The CALL has the general form

CALL name$(a_1, a_2, \ldots)$;

Here, the list $a_1, a_2, \ldots$ designates the arguments, which must be of the same type (numeric or string) as their corresponding parameters in the procedure's definition. For example, if we want to insert the string 'NEWb' immediately after the fifth position in the string variable SENT whose value is

```
EACH NEW PREPOSITION OPERATES SYNTACTICALLY .
```

then we would write the CALL statement

```
CALL INSERT (SENT, 'NEWb', 5);
```

And the resulting value of SENT will be changed as follows:

```
EACH NEW PREPOSITION OPERATES SYNTACTICALLY .
```

Note that the length of a string variable is affected by such an insertion *only* if it has the VARYING attribute.

Following are a number of other useful procedures that can be considered as a nucleus for text processing applications.

2-7.2 Substring Deletion

Given a string A and integers I and J, delete that substring from A that begins in position I and has length J.

```
DELETE: PROC(A,I,J);
    DCL A CHAR(*) VAR, (I,J) FIXED BIN;
    IF I > 0 & I <= LENGTH(A) & I+J-1 <= LENGTH(A)
    THEN A = SUBSTR(A,1,I-1) || SUBSTR(A,I+J);
    END DELETE;
```

For example, CALL DELETE (SENT,1,5) leaves the value of SENT as 'PREPOSITION OPERATES SYNTACTICALLY .'.

2-7.3 List Search

It is often helpful to search an array for the presence of a particular word. When an array of strings is used as a parameter, the parameter is declared as follows in the procedure:

```
DCL pi(*) CHAR(*) VAR;
```

If the array parameter has numbers, rather than strings, it is declared as follows:

```
DCL pi(*) FIXED BIN;
```

The following procedure searches the array of strings A for the presence of the string B. If B occurs in A, the parameter I is set to the subscript of the first occurrence of B in A. Otherwise, I is set to 0:

```
SEARCH: PROC(A,B,I);
    DCL (A(*),B) CHAR(*) VAR, (I,J) FIXED BIN;
    I = 0;
    DO J = 1 TO HBOUND(A,1) WHILE (A(J) ¬= '');
        IF A(J) = B THEN DO;
            I = J;
            RETURN;
            END;
        END;
    END SEARCH;
```

Here, the PL/I built-in function HBOUND(A,1) identifies the actual number of elements in the array A. This avoids using an additional parameter to identify that number. Here we also use the convention, established in a previous section, that the first occurrence of a null string in A will trigger exit from the loop. This speeds up the process of *not* finding a word in a large array that is only partially filled.

To illustrate, suppose we have the array WORDS declared and initialized as follows:

```
DCL WORDS(100) CHAR(30) VAR INIT(
    'EACH', 'PREPOSITION', 'OPERATES',
    'SYNTACTICALLY','');
```

The following CALL statement invokes a search of WORDS for an occurrence of 'OPERATES':

```
CALL SEARCH(WORDS,'OPERATES',K);
```

The result will be returned as the value of the variable K, which we assume has been declared as a numeric variable, as follows:

K | 3 |

K would have been set to 0 if OPERATES had not been among the words in WORDS.

Note also in this procedure that the auxiliary variable J controls the loop. Since it is declared within the procedure SEARCH, J is accessible only to the statements within SEARCH. Whenever control is outside the procedure, J is not accessible.

2-7.4   Pattern Matching

Often in text processing, we need to search a string for an occurrence of a particular pattern of characters. The simplest kind of pattern is a single-character string, and an effective search for it may be given directly by the INDEX built-in function.

A more complicated kind of pattern is one in which we are searching for any one of a number of alternative strings within a given string. For instance, we might be looking for the first occurrence of an article ('A', 'AN', or 'THE') within a sentence, and we do not particularly care which one we find.

This kind of function is not realizable in PL/I without adopting some convention for describing alternatives. We shall describe alternatives using an array ALTS. The last alternative in the array will be following by a null string (' '), which consequently prevents ' ' from being an alternative itself. The following procedure tries to match each alternative with a substring of the string in question, say A, beginning in position 1. If no match occurs, then the alternatives are all retried using a substring of A that begins in position 2. This process continues until either a match is found or all such substrings are tried without a match. The parameter I is set to either the position in A of the leftmost character of the substring for which a match is found, of 0 if no match is found. The parameter L designates the length of the matched string:

```
ALT: PROC (A,ALTS,I,L);
     DCL (A,ALTS(*)) CHAR(*) VAR, (I,J,K,L) FIXED
        BIN;
     I = 0; L = 0;
     DO J =1 TO LENGTH (A);
          DO K = 1 TO HBOUND(ALTS,1) WHILE
                (ALTS(K) ⌐ = '');
              IF J+LENGTH(ALTS(K)) <=
              LENGTH(A)+1
          THEN IF SUBSTR (A, J, LENGTH (ALTS (K))
                = ALTS (K))
              THEN DO;
              I = J;
              L = LENGTH(ALTS(K));
              RETURN;
              END;
          END;
        END;
     END ALT;
```

First, the reader should note that this is a fairly compact algorithm. It combines several techniques that were introduced above, and then imbeds them within a *tight* control structure. The alternatives in ALTS are taken in order, as specified by K. An alternative is only considered if its length permits a comparison substring of the same length to be defined beginning in position J of A. That is the purpose of the first IF statement within the inner DO loop.

To illustrate the use of this procedure, let us return to the problem of finding the first article within a sentence. Assume the following:

```
DCL SENT CHAR (300) VAR INIT
    ('ЂTHEЂOWLЂANDЂTHEЂPUSSYЂCATЂ.'),
    ARTICLE(3) CHAR(5) VAR INIT
    ('ЂAЂ', 'ЂANЂ', 'ЂTHEЂ'),
    (ARTPOS, ARTLEN) FIXED BIN;
  ⋮
CALL ALT(SENT, ARTICLE, ARTPOS, ARTLEN);
```

The result of executing the CALL statement will leave the values of ARTPOS and ARTLEN at 1 and 5, respectively, since the article 'ЂTHEЂ' appears in positions 1-5.

Notice that we are careful in specifying the list of alternatives when the alternatives are complete words. If we had initialized the ARTICLE array with the values 'A', 'AN', and 'THE' then the ALT procedure would not distinguish an occurrence of the word 'THE' from an occurrence of the string 'THE' within another word, such as 'OTHER'. The use of careful programming techniques tends to minimize errors that can occur from these kinds of pitfalls. This problem also helps to explain why the end-of-sentence period is preceded by a blank space.

2-8 Advanced Input and Output with Applications in Bibliographic Search and Dictionary Building

In Section 2-2, we discussed input and output operations as *stream* actions; the input and output data were viewed as continuous streams of values, extending from card to card and from line to line. Another way to view input and output is one in which each individual input card or output print line is treated as a separate entity, known as a *record*. This view is more useful than the earlier views when we need to access data stored on magnetic tape or disk. It is essential when we wish to access data randomly rather than sequentially.

Before discussing tape, disk, and random access input and output, we first introduce PL/I's facilities for describing data records. Next, we introduce the "record input and output" statements for reading and writing such data. Then, the notion of random access is introduced, and two important text processing applications are described: bibliographic search and dictionary building.

2-8.1 Describing Data Records

A *record* is a fixed number of characters stored on some computer-readable or writable medium, such as a punched card, a magnetic tape, or a magnetic disk. A *file* is a collection of such records. All the records in a file must reside on the same reel of tape, deck of cards, or disk pack, and all must have the same number[4] of characters. This number is known as the file's *record length*.

Unlike card files, different tape and disk files are not all required to have the same number of character positions. For instance, one file may have a record length of 160 characters and another may have a record length of 500 characters. The choice of record length for tape or disk files is often an arbitrary matter. Sometimes it is convenient to have a multiple of 80 as the record length; this facilitates transfer of the file's contents from cards to tape or disk, or vice versa. Also, the size of a line on the screen of most CRT terminals is 80 characters, and thus a record length of 80 facilitates visual display for the file.

The input and output of files as collections of records is known as *record I/O*. A basic characteristic of record I/O is that each input operation reads exactly one record from the file, and each output operation writes exactly one record to the file. Thus when data are read or written the program must have a variable that will accommodate an entire record. The simplest method is to define a CHARACTER variable whose length is the length of one record. For example, to read from a file whose record length is 100, we could declare a space for one record as

```
DCL REC CHAR(100);
```

This, however, is unsuitable if the file's records are formatted into *fields*. A field is a series of locations within a record, which contains a single data value, numeric or string. For example, suppose we wish to establish a file containing a bibliography. Each entry in the bibliography may be stored in a single 320-character record. The fields can be defined as follows:

Field positions	Contents
1-10	a 10-digit identifying number for the entry
11-80	the title of entry
81-160	the authors for the entry
161-240	other publishing information for the entry (publisher, date, journal, volume, etc.)
241-320	keywords for classifying the entry

[4] Other alternatives are beyond the scope of this book.

To declare space for a single record, and simultaneously to identify each field as a separate variable, PL/I provides the *structure*. A structure can be declared as follows:

```
DCL  1   structure-name,
     2 name attributes
     2 name attributes,
       ⋮
     2 name attributes;
```

Here, "structure-name" denotes the name by which the entire structure, or record, will be known, while each "name" denotes the name of an individual field within the record. Each "attributes" defines the attributes (e.g., CHARACTER) of its corresponding name just as if it were an ordinary variable.

For example, to declare a structure named BIBENTRY, which will accommodate an individual record from the file described above, we can write the following:

```
DCL  1 BIBENTRY,
       2 IDENT CHAR(10),
       2 TITLE CHAR(70),
       2 AUTHOR CHAR(80),
       2 PUBLICATION CHAR(80),
       2 KEYWORDS CHAR(80);
```

Record description structures can be written for any number of hierarchical levels. In the above example, only two levels of description are needed, one for the entire record and one for the individual fields. Suppose, however, that we wanted to further divide the author's name into "last name," "first name," and "initial," occupying positions 81-100, 101-115, and 116-120, respectively, and reserve positions 121-160 for specifying a second author's name in the same way. This can be done as follows:

```
DCL  1 BIBENTRY,
       2 IDENT CHAR(10),
       2 TITLE CHAR(70),
       2 AUTHOR1,
         3 LAST CHAR(20),
         3 FIRST CHAR(15),
         3 MIDDLE CHAR(5),
       2 AUTHOR2,
         3 LAST CHAR(20),
         3 FIRST CHAR(15),
         3 MIDDLE CHAR(5),
```

```
2 PUBLICATION CHAR(80),
2 KEYWORDS CHAR(80);
```

Note that more than one occurrence of the variable names LAST, FIRST, and MIDDLE appears. This is permissible, provided that the two names can be distinguished by having different names at some higher level in the structure. That is, the first occurrence of LAST has AUTHOR1 at a higher level, while the second occurrence of LAST has AUTHOR2 at a higher level. Whenever we want to reference the first variable named LAST, we qualify it by writing AUTHOR1.LAST. The second variable LAST is identified as AUTHOR2.LAST. In this way, the value of AUTHOR1.LAST is unique and distinguishable from the value of AUTHOR2.LAST.

A slightly simpler approach to the question of multiple occurrences of a field within a record can be achieved by the use of arrays. We can treat any structure (or substructure) as an array by simply attaching a dimension to it. For example, the above declaration of BIBENTRY can alternatively be written

```
DCL 1 BIBENTRY,
       2 IDENT CHAR(10),
       2 TITLE CHAR(70),
       2 AUTHOR(2),
          3 LAST CHAR(20),
          3 FIRST CHAR(15),
          3 MIDDLE CHAR(5),
       2 PUBLICATION CHAR(80),
       2 KEYWORDS CHAR(80);
```

When this is done, all variables at lower levels in the hierarchy inherit the given dimensions. In this example, for instance, the variables LAST, FIRST, and MIDDLE inherit the dimension 2. Thus, the first author's LAST name is given by LAST(1) while the second author's last name is given by LAST(2).

2-8.2 Sequential Record Input and Output

To perform input and output operations on a file as a series of records, the READ and WRITE statements are used. Throughout this section we discuss READ and WRITE statements as they apply to sequential input and output. In the next section, we turn our attention to reading and writing the records of a file in a nonsequential or random manner.

The READ statement, when executed, causes transfer of one record from a file into a variable or structure. The form of the READ statement is

```
READ FILE(filename) INTO (record);
```

Here, "filename" identifies the file and "record" identifies the variable or structure into which the record is to be stored.

Like a variable name, a filename is made up of letters and digits, the first of which must be a letter. IBM implementations limit the length of filenames to a maximum of eight characters.

There are two filenames that are already provided with PL/I: the standard system input file SYSIN, and the standard system print file SYSPRINT. We have already seen occurrences of these filenames in the conditions ENDFILE(SYSIN) and ENDPAGE(SYSPRINT). In fact, ENDFILE(filename) can appear in an ON statement for *any* input file.

Suppose that we want to read and print the bibliography file whose records were defined above, according to the following print layout:

1–40	41–80	81–90
author 1	author 2	ident
title		
publication		
keywords		

Here, four lines are required for each entry and there should be a blank line between adjacent entries.

The following program reads the records from this file, which we shall call BIBFILE, and prints them in the above format.

```
BIBLIST: PROC OPTION(MAIN);
DCL 1 BIBENTRY,
     2 IDENT CHAR(10),
     2 TITLE CHAR(70),
     2 AUTHOR(2) CHAR(40),
     2 PUBLICATION CHAR(80),
     2 KEYWORDS CHAR(80);
ON ENDFILE (BIBFILE) STOP;
DO WHILE('1'B);
   READ FILE (BIBFILE) INTO (BIBENTRY);
   PUT EDIT (AUTHOR, IDENT, TITLE, PUBLICATION,
     KEYWORDS)
     (A,A,A,3 (COL(1),A));
   PUT SKIP(2);
   END;
END BIBLIST;
```

The program should be self-explanatory, with the exception of a detail in the PUT statement. There, we wrote AUTHOR instead of AUTHOR(1), AU–

THOR(2). This is always permissible for arrays in GET and PUT statements, provided that a sufficient number of format items are present to accommodate all the array's entries. Further, if the individual variables in the structure BI-BENTRY are to be printed in the same order in which they are declared, then the PUT statement can be written with one name, BIBENTRY, instead of all its variable's names. In this case, too, the format list must accommodate the number of individual data values to be printed.

To output a record to a file, the WRITE statement can be used. It has the form

WRITE FILE(filename) FROM(record);

The meanings of "filename" and "record" are the same here as for the READ statement.

Suppose, for example, that we want to create the bibliography file on magnetic tape, assuming that the individual entries are punched on cards as follows:

Card	Contents		
	1–10	11–40	41–80
1	ident	title	
2	author1		author2
3	publication		
4	keywords		

The following program creates that file, and in the process performs certain validity checks on the card data:

```
BIBTAPE: PROC OPTIONS (MAIN);
        DCL 1   BIBENTRY,
                2 IDENT CHAR(10),
                2 TITLE CHAR(70),
                2 AUTHOR(2) CHAR(40),
                2 PUBLICATION CHAR(80),
                2 KEYWORDS CHAR(80);
        DCL I   FIXED BIN;
        ON ENDFILE(SYSIN) STOP;
            DO I = 1 BY 1;
                GET EDIT (BIBENTRY) (A(10), A(70),
                    2 A(40), 2 A(80));
                IF VERIFY (IDENT, '0123456789' ¬= 0
                    THEN GO TO ERR;
                IF TITLE = "|AUTHOR(1) = " THEN GO
                    TO ERR;
```

```
          WRITE FILE (BIBFILE) FROM (BIBENTRY);
          END;
     ERR: PUT EDIT ('ERROR INPUT, RUN CANCELLED')
                   (A);
     END BIBTAPE;
```

This program checks that IDENT is wholly numeric and that neither TITLE nor AUTHOR(1) is blank. The reader should also note that other kinds of errors can occur that will go unchecked, such as spelling errors. Also, suppose an author card and a keywords card become reversed, or the last entry in the deck has fewer than four cards. Neither of these errors will be checked by the program.

An important characteristic of the last two programs is that they will be effective whether the bibliography file is on tape or on disk. To select tape or disk as the I/O medium requires specifications outside the PL/I language. The reader should learn the conventions that are in use at his/her installation. Appendix B gives the rudiments of tape and disk I/O for most IBM 360 and 370 installations.

The principal application of bibliographic data processing is the search for entries that have one or more of a specified list of keywords. The program that performs the search has the following tasks:

(1) Identify the keywords that will control the search.
(2) Read a record from the bibliographic file.
(3) Search its KEYWORDS portion to find an instance of one of the controlling keywords.
(4) If one is found, print the entire record.
(5) Repeat steps 2-4 until the file is exhausted.

This application uses much of the information that we have already presented in this chapter, and so we present only the skeleton of its solution below. The reader will be asked to complete the program as an exercise.

The program will be organized as two auxiliary procedures and a main procedure. The auxiliary procedures will have as their function the following:

Procedure	Function
CONTROL	Identify the keywords that will control the search and place them in the array CONTROLS; a maximum of 30 different keywords can be entered on cards, and the actual number entered will be stored in the variable NC.
SCREEN	Read a record from BIBFILE and determine whether or not one of its KEYWORDS is among the NC keywords in CONTROLS. If so, the switch SELECTED is set to '1'B. Otherwise, SELECTED is set to '0'B.

The program can thus be organized as follows:

```
BIBSRCH: PROC OPTIONS (MAIN);
          DCL  1 BIBENTRY,
               2 IDENT CHAR(10),
               2 TITLE CHAR(70),
               2 AUTHOR(2) CHAR(40),
               2 PUBLICATION CHAR(80),
               2 KEYWORDS CHAR(80);
          DCL  CONTROLS(30) CHAR(30) VAR,
               NC FIXED BIN,
               SELECTED BIT(1);
CONTROL: PROC;
             ⋮
     END CONTROL;
SCREEN: PROC;
             ⋮
     END SCREEN;
  ON ENDFILE (BIBFILE) STOP;
  CALL CONTROL;
  DO I = 1 BY 1;
     CALL SCREEN;
     IF SELECTED THEN PUT EDIT (BIBENTRY) (SKIP, 6 A);
     END;
END BIBSRCH;
```

2-8.3 *Nonsequential Record Input and Output*

Until now we have treated files sequentially, i.e., one record at a time beginning with the first. Such a treatment usually simplifies the programming task. Sometimes, however, it prevents effective realization of the program and we are forced to consider a more general method.

The most common application of text processing that requires a nonsequential input and output method is the dictionary search. That is, given a word either find it in the dictionary or determine that it is not present. For the program to perform a *sequential* search of the dictionary, particularly when it contains several thousand entries, is as ineffective as if we were asked to look up a word in an ordinary printed dictionary by starting at the first page and scanning each page until either we find the word or we exhaust the dictionary.

Because a computer dictionary usually contains several thousand entries, it must be treated as a disk file rather than an array in memory. To access such a file nonsequentially, each record must have associated with it a special field known as the record's *key*. The key has the characteristic that it distinguishes its record from other records in the file. Thus, the various keys in a file must all be different. For a file that is a dictionary, each individual word is the natural choice for the key. Consider the following declaration for a dictionary record:

```
DLC 1 DICRCD,
     2 DEL CHAR (1),
     2 WORD CHAR (30),
     2 PART_OF_SPEECH CHAR (3),
     2 NUMBER CHAR (1),
     2 MEANING CHAR (45);
```

Here, the PART_OF_SPEECH may be coded as 'N' for noun, 'ADJ' for adjective, and so forth. The NUMBER is coded 'S' for singular and 'P' for plural, and the MEANING contains a brief definition for the WORD.

The purpose of DEL is as follows. A nonsequential file is always stored in magnetic disk rather than some sequential medium, because its records are accessed randomly. The disk is the only medium that can accommodate this method of accessing a file. Such a file is called an INDEXED file. Each record in the file resides in a particular location on the disk. The actual mechanism and logic by which records are stored and retrieved from a disk file are beyond the scope of this text. However, that mechanism requires that the first character (DEL) of each record be reserved for exclusive use by the system,[5] i.e., it cannot be manipulated by the program in any way. Thus, we define DEL in the record declaration and then ignore it in the program.

To read or write a record in an INDEXED file, the following statements can be used:

```
READ FILE (filename) INTO (record) KEY (keyname);
WRITE FILE (filename) FROM (record) KEYFROM (keyname);
```

The INDEXED file itself must be declared in a so-called file declaration as follows:

```
DCL filename FILE DIRECT KEYED ⎧INPUT ⎫;
                                ⎨OUTPUT⎬
                                ⎩UPDATE⎭
```

For a file declared as INPUT, only the READ statement can be used. For OUTPUT only the WRITE statement can be used. However, when a file is declared for UPDATE, the READ statement can be used to read a record and the WRITE statement can be used to write a new record. In addition, the UPDATE mode permits the following two additional input/output operations:

---

[5] This discussion is implementation dependent.

DELETE FILE (filename) KEY (keyname);
REWRITE FILE (filename) FROM (record) KEYFROM (keyname);

The DELETE statement causes the record with the designated "keyname" to be deleted from the file, and the REWRITE statement causes the record most recently read to be rewritten (replaced) in the file.

Whenever these input/output operations are specified, there is the possibility that the designated action can be fulfilled. This is due to the presence or absence of a record, with the same key, in the file at the time the operation occurs. The following summarizes those unusual events:

Operation	Event	ON–code
READ DELETE REWRITE	No record with the desired key is in the file.	51
WRITE	A record with the same key is already in the file.	52

The "ON–codes" listed on the right are actual values for the system-defined variable ONCODE when the indicated events actually occur. Furthermore, any of these events will cause the "KEY condition" to be raised for the file in question. To deal with these events in a program, one writes an ON statement of the form

ON KEY (filename) BEGIN;

                    .

                    .

                    .

                    END;

For an INPUT or OUTPUT file, the value of ONCODE need not be interrogated to determine how the condition was raised. For an UPDATE file, however, there may be READ, WRITE, DELETE, and REWRITE statements in the program. To distinguish what kind of statement was executing when the KEY condition actually occurred, the value of ONCODE should be interrogated within the ON statement itself.

To illustrate the use of nonsequential input and output, we present a simple dictionary-building exercise using the record layout given above. We have a dictionary, and we wish to perform a series of additions, deletions, and changes to it. Each addition, deletion of change is punched on a card in the following way:

Column	Contents
1	code: A, addition: C, change, D, deletion
2-31	the WORD itself
32-34	its PART_OF_SPEECH
35	its NUMBER
36-80	its MEANING

The update cards are not necessarily in alphabetical order. Here is a group of example updates, together with an example dictionary (before the updates are actually made):

Updates				
A	RHINO	N	S	AN ANIMAL
C	BAD	ADJ		NOT GOOD
C	MONKEY	N	S	AN ANIMAL
D	BELT			
A	NICE	ADJ		PLEASANT
D	BROWN			

Dictionary (before the updates are made)			
BAD	N	S	
BELT	N	S	PRECISE AMOUNT OF WHISKEY
MONKEY	V		TO CLOWN AROUND
NICE	ADJ		PLEASANT
PURPLE	ADJ		A COLOR

After the updates are made, the resulting dictionary will be changed as follows:

Dictionary (after the updates are made)			
BAD	ADJ		NOT GOOD
MONKEY	N	S	AN ANIMAL
NICE	ADJ		PLEASANT
PURPLE	ADJ		A COLOR
RHINO	N	S	AN ANIMAL

Note here that a "change" means that a record with a given key (BAD in this case) may have one or more of its fields changed, but not the key itself. Note also that not all updates can necessarily be performed. Here, NICE cannot be added because a record with the same key is already in the dictionary, and BROWN cannot be deleted because there is no record with that key in the dictionary. The following program performs updates of this kind to the dictionary.

```
UPDAT: PROC OPTIONS (MAIN);
      DCL DIC FILE DIRECT KEYED UPDATE;
      DCL   1 DICRCD,
               2 DEL CHAR (1),
               2 WORD CHAR (30),
               2 REST CHAR (49),
             1 UPDATE,
               2 UTYPE CHAR (1),
               2 UWORD CHAR (30),
               2 UREST CHAR (49);
ON ENDFILE(SYSIN) STOP;
ON KEY (DIC) GO TO GETNEXT;
GETNEXT: GET EDIT (UPDATE) (A(1),A(30),A(49));
      IF UTYPE = 'A'
      THEN WRITE FILE (DIC) FROM (UPDATE) KEYFROM
           (UWORD);
      ELSE IF UTYPE = 'C' THEN DO;
             READ FILE (DIC) INTO (DICRCD) KEY (UWORD);
             REWRITE FILE (DIC) FROM (UPDATE) KEY
                     (UWORD);
             END;
             ELSE IF UTYPE = 'D' THEN DELETE FILE (DIC)
                  KEY (UWORD);
      GO TO GETNEXT;
END UPDAT;
```

The reader should see that, although this program performs the task, it is not a particularly practical one. For example, when an update is in error for some reason or other, a useful program would print it and a message indicating the nature of the error. This and other refinements to the update program will be left as exercises.

2-9   Hints for Diagnosing Errors in PL/I Programs: SUBRG, STRG, and Program Trace

Inevitably, the programmer faces the task of making a program work correctly, as well as protecting it from becoming inoperative due to the presence of invalid data. *This task, known as debugging or program verification, takes a lot of practice to reach a high level of proficiency.* Here, we present some of the PL/I language facilities that aid in the task of program debugging. Specifically, we illustrate the use of SUBRG, STRG, and CHECK features.

SUBRG, which is short for "subscriptrange," is a condition that is raised when an array reference is outside the range of correct subscript values. For example, if we delcare an array WORDS as

DCL WORDS(100) CHAR(30) VAR,

the only correct subscripts are integers from 1 to 100. If we write WORDS(203) or WORDS(I) with I having some value not in the range from 1 to 100, then the SUBRG condition will be raised.

Unlike the other (input/output) conditions that we have discussed, the SUBRG condition is in a so-called disabled state unless the programmer explicitly "enables" it.[6] That is, SUBRG will not be raised when a subscript is out of range unless it has been enabled. Indeed, unknown and unpredictable side effects may be produced by this event and program execution can continue as if nothing happened. To enable SUBRG means to elevate it to the same status as the other (input/output) conditions, that is, to allow it to be raised when an invalid subscript actually occurs.

Enabling a condition is accomplished by prefixing the program with the condition name, enclosed in parentheses, and followed by a colon as shown:

(condition name):
program name: PROC OPTIONS (MAIN);
     ⋮
     END program name;

Several conditions may be enabled in this way by listing them, separated by commas, within the parentheses.

STRG, which is short for "stringrange," is a condition raised when a SUBSTR specification describes a string that is not, in fact, a substring of a given string. For example, each of the following will cause the STRG condition to be raised:

SUBSTR ('EACH', 1, 24)
SUBSTR ('EACH', 0, 1)
SUBSTR ('EACH', 2, -1)

In the first case, the length of the substring exceeds the length of the given string 'EACH'. In the second, the starting position is invalid, and in the third, the negative length is invalid. [Note that a substring of length 0 is valid at any position in the given string. The result is the null string (").] Like SUBRG, the STRG condition is also initially disabled, and can be enabled by prefixing it to the program as shown above. Failure to do so will cause occurrences of STRG to be passed undetected, and unpredictable events may follow.

---

[6] This information is implementation dependent.

It is good practice to initially enable all conditions that can occur while a program is being developed and debugged. Whether or not an ON statement is provided for each condition is optional. If an ON statement is not present for an enabled condition and if that condition is actually raised, program execution will be interrupted and a message will be printed that identifies both the condition and the statement in the program that caused the condition to be raised.

The most powerful and versatile debugging aid in PL/I is its "CHECK condition". It enables tracing of the succession of values that a variable takes, as well as the succession of statement labels and/or procedure names that are executed. The CHECK condition is enabled by writing the following condition within the program's prefix:

CHECK(names)

Here, "names" denotes a list of variable names, procedure names, and/or statement lables whose values are to be traced. Each time one of the named variables is assigned a value (by an assignment statement or an input statement), its name and value are printed in the following form:

name = value;

Each time one of the named procedures is called (or one of the named statement labels is executed), its name (or label) will be printed. Therefore, the results that are printed show a complete execution history of the values of the named variables, procedures, and/or labels, in the order in which the events actually took place.

To illustrate these facilities, consider the following problem. We would like to write a procedure that sorts alphabetically a list of words that are punched on cards, and then prints the sorted list. The program calls the procedure SORTWDS, whose purpose is to sort an array of N words. The words are assumed to be stored on individual cards, each beginning in column 1:

```
SORTPGM: PROC OPTIONS (MAIN);
         DCL WORDS (100) CHAR (30) VAR, CARD CHAR (80),
             (I,J) FIXED BIN;
         SORTWDS: PROC (WDS, N);
             DCL WDS(*) CHAR(*) VAR,
                 N FIXED BIN;
                 .
                 .
                 .
             END SORTWDS;
         ON ENDFILE(SYSIN) GO TO SORTEM;
         /* READ AND COUNT THE WORDS IN I*/
```

```
DO I = 0 BY 1;
    GET EDIT (CARD) (A(80));
    J = INDEX(CARD, 'b')-1;
    WORDS(I+1) = SUBSTR(CARD,1,J);
    END;
SORTEM: CALL SORTWDS (WORDS, I);
    /* PRINT THE SORTED WORDS */
    DO J = 1 to I;
            PUT SKIP LIST (WORDS(J));
            END;
END SORTPGM;
```

Usually, this program works correctly. However, whenever the data are not just right, the program goes awry. We would like to find out the cause of this behavior and change the program so that it is better protected against such events. First, note that the program can accommodate no more than 100 words (input cards). Second, note that it assumes each word is properly entered on a card, that it is no longer than 30 characters, and that there are no blank cards in the input.

To trap such behavior, we can prefix the program with the following:

```
(STRG, SUBRG, CHECK(I,J,CARD,SORTWDS)):
```

Now any occurrence of an invalid SUBSTR operation or subscript out of range will be detected, and at that point the current values of the variables I, J, and CARD will have been printed. With that information, the program can be revised to protect itself from occurrences of invalid data.

Question and Exercises

1. What is the purpose of variables in PL/I? Declarations?

2. Write a suitable declaration for each of the following variables:

(a) A counter named I whose values will be strictly integers.

(b) A character string named NAME whose value will be a person's last name, containing at most 20 characters.

(c) A location named COST, which will contain the dollars-and-cents cost of a computer, at most $99,999,999.99.

3. What is the advantage of arrays?

4. Declare an array called NAMES, which can hold up to 100 persons' last names, when it is known also that no name will exceed 20 characters in length.

5. (a) Write a GET statement that will read the two names given below into the first two entries of the array NAMES declared above (question 4):

```
  'FOCAULT'                 'JAMES'
```

(b)   Do the same when the names are instead given as follows:

col   1   10   70
```
                             FOCAULT       JAMES
```

6. (a)   Summarize the effects when the precision of a numeric variable is different from the number of digits in a numeric value that is read and stored in that variable.

(b)   Show what will be stored in the variable PCT, declared as FIXED DEC (5,2), for each of the following input data values:

(i)   17.5

(ii)   17.521

(iii)   −0.25

7. (a)   Summarize the effects when the length of a string variable is different from that of a string that is read and stored in that variable.

(b)   Show what will be stored in the variable STR, declared as CHAR−ACTER(5), for each of the following input data values:

(i)   'SUN'

(ii)   'SUNNY'

(iii)   'SUNNYVALE'

8. Write a PUT statement that prints the array WORDS (shown in Section 2-2) in each of the following ways:

(a)   All four entries on one line, at tab positions 1, 31, 61, and 91, respectively.

(b)   All four entries in a column, at tab position 53.

(c)   All four entries in reverse order, in a column at tab position 1.

9. Given the variables and values

```
  I      3   J    7        AMT   1.25   SUM   37.2
```

Show what will be stored for each variable on the left of the following assignment statements:

(a)   H = I+3*J;   (assume H is FIXED BIN)

(b)   Q = (I*AMT − SUM/3)*J**2;   (assume Q is FIXED DEC (7,2))

(c)   AMT = AMT/2;   (assume AMT is FIXED DEC (3,1))

10. Show how an assignment can be used for each of the following purposes:

(a)   Set all the entries in the array COUNTERS (declared as an array of 12 FIXED BIN values) to zero.

(b) Compute the sum of the first three entries in COUNTERS and store that sum in the fourth entry.

11. Repeat question 10a using the INITIAL attribute rather than an assignment statement.

12. What is the purpose of control statements in a PL/I program?

13. Let S, T, and U be string variables, and A, B, and C be numeric variables. Write an IF statement that will increment the value of I (i.e., increase I by 1) when each of the following conditions is true:

    (a) S and T are the same string.
    (b) S is a blank string, and T and U are not identical.
    (c) The sum of the values of A and B is greater than the product of the values of B and C.
    (d) B is not zero and either S is blank or T is blank.

14. Write a DO statement for each of the following:

    (a) Count the number of occurrences of 'A', 'AN', and 'THE' collectively within the array WORDS, declared as
    DCL WORDS(100) CHAR(30) VAR;
    and initialized with values elsewhere in the program.
    (b) Print the words in this array in reverse order, beginning with WORDS(100).
    (c) Print the words in this array in reverse order, but only until a blank word is reached.

15. Complete the program PGM2 in Section 2-4 by writing the procedures READER and PRINTER identified there. Assume that each sentence is on one or more cards and ends with a period. Assume also that each sentence begins in column 1 of a new card. For output, PRINTER should print each sentence beginning on a new line, followed by a message that identifies the number of occurrences 'THE' within the sentence. That message should be printed on the next line after the end of the sentence and followed by a blank line.

16. Illustrate the ease of program modification that procedures permit by altering PGM2 (Section 2-4) in the following way: for each sentence, print the message that identifies its number of 'THE's *only* if it contains one or more 'THE's. Otherwise, print only the sentence, followed by a blank line.

17. Alter PGM3 in Section 2-4 so that it lists a deck of cards *without* a heading at the top of each page, but counts and prints on a separate page the *number* of cards that were listed.

18. Show what results from each of the following concatenation and substring expressions, assuming that the variables S and T are delcared and initialized as

```
DCL (S INIT( 'THEREFORE,...'),
     T INIT ('THE')) CHAR(30) VAR;
```

(a) S ‖ T

(b) T ‖ 'ƀ' ‖ 'DOG'

(c) SUBSTR(S,1,9),

(d) SUBSTR(S,11) ‖ T ‖ SUBSTR(S,4,3)

19. Show what will result if each of the expressions in question 18 is placed on the right of an assignment statement with the variable U on the left. U is defined as
DCL U CHAR (10);

20. Modify the algorithm in Section 2-6, which stores the individual words from SENT in WORDS, so that it will print a message and stop execution if a sentence is encountered that contains more than 100 words.

21. Using the procedures INSERT, DELETE, SEARCH, and ALTS defined in Section 2-7, write PL/I statements that will accomplish the following:

(a)   Delete all occurrences of THE in the sentence SENT.

(b)   Add S to the end of each word in SENT.

(c)   Replace each occurrence of the article A or AN in the sentence SENT by the article THE.

In each of these SENT should be assumed to be declared as CHAR(300) VAR, and to already contain a string value. Furthermore, each of these solutions should leave the *same* spacing between words that it found.

22. Complete the program BIBSRCH in Section 2-8 by writing the procedures CONTROL and SCREEN.

23. Improve the dictionary UPDATE program in Section 2-8 by adding statements that:

(a)   Count the number of additions, changes, and deletions made in a particular run.

(b)   Edit each update for validity by checking for a nonblank UWORD and (for additions) nonblank part of speech and meaning. Print an error message for each error update that is detected, and then continue to process the next update.

24. Write the procedure SORTWDS that was identified in the program SORTPGM of Section 2-9.

25. Using the hints at the end of Section 2-9, revise the program SORTPGM to protect itself against occurrences of words that either begin past column 1 or exceed 30 characters in length. Each such card should be printed by the program and excluded from the sort process.

Chapter 3

Introduction to SNOBOL for Text Processing

Unlike PL/I, SNOBOL was designed specifically as a text processing language. As we discuss the SNOBOL programming features, we shall see that it contains more extensive text processing capabilities than PL/I. On the other hand, SNOBOL's file manipulation capabilities are relatively limited, since they are derived from FORTRAN. Nevertheless, the overall capability of SNOBOL in text processing is quite powerful.

3-1 Numbers, Strings, Variables, and Arrays

The main data type in SNOBOL is the *string*. When appearing within a program, a string, is enclosed in apostrophes (') or quotes ("), and consists of zero or more characters from among the following:

```
ƀ  .  (  +  &  !  $  *  )  ;  -  /  ,  %  ?  :  #  @  '  =  "
A  B  C  D  E  F  G  H  I  J  K  L  M  N  O  P  Q  R  S  T  U  V  W  X  Y  Z
0  1  2  3  4  5  6  7  8  9
```

When a *number* appears within a program, it may be written without enclosing quotes. It is written in the ordinary way, with or without a decimal point or sign. Below are some examples of numbers and strings in SNOBOL:

Strings	Numbers
'ABC'	-1.73
'AƀBƀC'	0
' '	37
"WHAT'SƀTHIS?"	.00025

Here, the first two strings are not equivalent in any sense; blanks (ƀ) are always significant when they are embedded within strings. The size of a string is its number of characters, excluding its enclosing quotes or apostrophe.

3-1.1 Variables

A SNOBOL *variable* is the means by which values (i.e., numbers and strings) can be stored in the memory, and thus analyzed and manipulated by the program. A variable has two parts, a "name" and a "memory location" that contains a value. The following notation is used throughout the chapter to denote a variable:

name | value |

The programmer assigns the variable's name and should choose one that tends to describe the purpose of the variable.

For example, we may have a variable whose value is the number of words in a sentence and another whose value is a sentence itself. Appropriately, we may choose to name these variables NWORDS and SENT, respectively.

The *value* of a variable may either be a number or a string. Furthermore, a variable's value will typically change at different times during program execution. For example, the values of SENT and NWORDS may, at one time during execution, be

SENT | EACHƀPREPOSITIONƀOPERATESƀSYNTACTICALLYƀ. |

NWORDS | 4 |

A variable can never contain more than one value at any one time. However, the type of value (number or string) may change. Thus, for example, the variable SENT shown above may at a later time contain the numeric value 4, rather than the string value shown above. That is, a variable's type is dynamic during program execution.

A variable *exists* in a SNOBOL program merely by virtue of its use, or appearance, within the program. No explicit declaration is required, as in the case of PL/I.

3-1.2 Arrays

It is often useful in programming to identify, by the same name, a series of memory locations that can each contain a separate value. For instance, we might like to store in separate locations the different words of a sentence. If variables are used for this purpose, we must assign a separate name to each memory location, as shown in the following example:

WORD1 | EACH |

WORD2 | PREPOSITION |

WORD3 | OPERATES |

WORD4 | SYNTACTICALLY |

More typically, a sentence will contain many more than four words, and the naming problem thus becomes difficult.

The *array* is designed to eliminate this naming problem. An array is a sequence of memory locations that share a single name. They are distinguished from each other by the attachment of a "subscript" at the right of the name. To define an array in SNOBOL, the following declaration must appear:

name = ARRAY<n>

This says literally that an array of n locations is to be created, and it will have the name "name." For example, the declaration

WORDS = ARRAY <100>

creates an array named WORDS of 100 memory locations. Below we show how the four words from the example sentence could be stored in the first four locations of WORDS:

WORDS

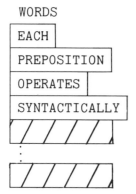

Here, the hatched areas indicate unused locations in WORDS.

To reference any one of these locations, a subscript is appended to WORDS. For example, the first location is reference as WORDS<1>, the second as WORDS< 2>, and so forth. Furthermore, if I (say) is a variable with an integer value from 1 to 100, then the expression WORDS<I> references the Ith location in WORDS. The array is a very powerful device, and we use it frequently throughout this chapter.

3-2   Elementary Input and Output

Now that we have variables and arrays for storing data values in memory, we introduce SNOBOL facilities that will bring values into these locations from external medium, as well as write values from these locations to an external medium, that is, perform "input" and "output" operations.

In this chapter, we only consider input on punched cards (or punched card images), and output on the printed page. A punched card contains exactly 80 characters, while a printed page usually contains 60 lines and 132 characters per line.[1] Input data are usually punched in cards in a free-form manner, from left to right, as shown below:

```
EACH PREPOSITION OPERATES SYNTACTICALLY  .
```

To transfer the contents of a *single* data card to a variable in memory, the following SNOBOL statement can be used:

name = INPUT

When this statement is executed, the entire 80-character contents of the card (including all blanks) become the value of the variable named "name." For instance, the statement

SENT = INPUT

leaves SENT with the following value, for the data card shown above:

SENT   `EACH PREPOSITION OPERATES SYNTACTICALLY  .`

Many times, we would like to store in a variable only the nonblank initial portion of a card, and "trim off" all trailing blanks from the right end. We can do this by saying TRIM(INPUT) instead of INPUT in the above statement. That is, the effect of

SENT = TRIM(INPUT)

is to leave the following in SENT:

SENT   `EACH PREPOSITION OPERATES SYNTACTICALLY  .`

To print a variable's value on the next line of the printed page, the following statement can be used:

OUTPUT = name

---

[1] This will vary among different computers and operating systems.

Here, "name" identifies the variable whose value is to be printed. For instance:

```
OUTPUT  =  SENT
```

will cause the value of SENT to be printed on the next line.

3-3   Expressions and Assignment

The input and output statements presented in the foregoing section are special instances of a more general class, called *assignment statements,* which have the following form:

name = expression

The "name" on the left denotes any variable or array reference, that serves to identify a single memory location. The "expression" on the right identifies a value, numeric or string, that will be placed in the named memory location when the statement is executed.

In its simplest form, the expression is merely a value or another variable or array reference (which identifies a value). For instance, the assignment

```
N  =  0
```

leaves N with the value of 0:

N $\boxed{0}$

The assignment

```
WORDS<1>  =  'EACH'
```

leaves the value of 'EACH' in the *first* entry of the array named WORDS:

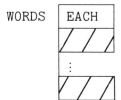

The expression on the right of an assignment can also specify one or more arithmetic calculations. For example, the assignment

```
N  =  N+1
```

literally says, "compute the sum N + 1 and then assign the result to N. If the value of N is initially 0, then the result will be as follows:

N $\boxed{1}$

The SNOBOL arithmetic operations are as follows:

Operation	Meaning
+	Addition
−	Subtraction
*	Multiplication
/	Division
**	Exponentiation

More than one arithmetic operation can occur within an assignment. If, for example, we want to calculate the average of the variables M and N and assign the result to a variable AV, then we could write the following:

AV = (M+N)/2

Notice here that we have enclosed the sum M + N within parentheses. That is done to force the order of arithmetic calculations so that the addition is done before the division. Without parentheses, the division N/2 would have been performed first, yielding a different result.

In general, an expression that contains *no* parentheses and more than one arithmetic operator will have its operations performed in the following order of priority:

(1)   All exponentiations (**), from right to left (if there are more than one).
(2)   All multiplications (*) and divisions (/), from left to right.
(3)   All additions (+) and subtractions (−), from left to right.

Whenever this defined order is not desired, parentheses should be inserted to designate the correct order.

The following expressions together with their algebraic equivalents on the right, should illustrate the effect of parenthesization on the order of calculation:

Expression	Algebraic equivalent
(M+N)/2	$\dfrac{M+N}{2}$
M+N/2	$M+\dfrac{N}{2}$
M+N/2*A	$M+\dfrac{NA}{2}$
M+N/(2*A)	$M+\dfrac{N}{2A}$

3-3.1   String-Valued Expressions

Expressions may also be written to construct *string* values, rather than calculate numerical values. The most common string operation in SNOBOL programming is *concatenation,* which simply constructs on string out of two. It is designated by placing the two strings side by side, separated by a blank space. For instance, the string 'ABCDEF' that results from concatenation of 'ABC' and 'DEF' is written as the following expression:

'ABC'ƀ'DEF'

To assign this value to a variable, say S, we can write the following assignment statement:

S = 'ABC' 'DEF'

Concatenation can also be designated for variables or other string expressions, as well as for two string constants. For instance, suppose S and T have the values

S | ABCDEF |

T | GHI |

Then the following assignments will affect U as shown on the right:

	Result value of U
U = S T	ABCDEFGHI
U = S 'ƀ'	'ABCDEFƀ'
U = TRIM(S 'ƀ')	'ABCDEF'

Note in the last example that the function TRIM is used to delete trailing blanks from the string value 'ABCDEFƀ'. When a function, such as TRIM is used this way, its argument (such as S 'ƀ') may be any expression. That expression is evaluated *before* the function is applied.

3-3.2   Array Initialization

To initialize *all* entries in an array to the *same* value, the array declaration can be written as follows:

name = ARRAY <n, value>

Here, "n" again denotes the size of the array, and "value" denotes the value to be stored in all of its entries. For example,

A = ARRAY <100,0>

declares A to be an array of 100 entries, and all entries have the initial value of 0. Later in the program, some or all of these initial values may change.

3-4 Complete Programs and Control Statements

A complete SNOBOL program may contain any sequence of statements, including array declarations, assignment statements, input and output statements, and others introduced in later sections, all followed by the final statement END. Immediately after the END statement, which marks the physical end of the program text, may be any data that are used as input by the program. (Additional control cards will be needed, both before the SNOBOL program and after the last data card. The specific contents will differ for different computers. The reader is urged to obtain this information for his/her own installation.)

The following example illustrates the general structure of SNOBOL programs. Its purpose is to read a single input data card, determine the number N of characters in the card up to its rightmost nonblank character, and then print the card's contents and the value of N:

```
*THIS PROGRAM READS A CARD, PRINTS IT AND
*THE SIZE OF ITS LEADING NONBLANK PORTION
      S = TRIM(INPUT)
      N = SIZE(S)
      OUTPUT = S
      OUTPUT = 'THE SIZE OF S = ' N
END
HERE IS THE DATA CARD.
```

The output that will be printed by this program is shown below:

```
HERE IS THE DATA CARD.
THE SIZE OF S = 22
```

As the first two lines of this program suggest, a *comment* line may be inserted anywhere within a SNOBOL that some explanatory remarks would be helpful to the reader. The asterisk (*) character is used to denote a comment line, and it must appear in the first position.

The END statement must also appear in the first position of its line. Any input data that will be applied to the program should immediately follow the END statement. All other statements in the program must be indented *beyond* the first position of its line. The first position is reserved for the placement of a statement *label*, which is discussed below.

The statements of a SNOBOL program are executed in the order in which they are written, beginning with the first, unless explicitly directed otherwise from within the program itself. Such directions are made by a so-called go to part, which can be appended on the right end of *any* SNOBOL statement. The go to part identifies, by its label, the statement that should be executed next.

A statement label may be any sequence of letters and/or digits, the first being a letter, that begins in position 1 of a line. The following statement, for instance, has the label L:

```
L  S  =  TRIM( INPUT )
```

Note also that a label must be separated from its statement by at least one blank space.

The execution of any SNOBOL statement is said to *succeed* or *fail,* depending upon the success or failure of execution for its constituent parts. Some statements generally succeed, by their nature, such as the following:

```
N  =  SIZE( S )
OUTPUT  =  S
```

However, other statements will fail under certain circumstances. For example, the statement

```
S  =  TRIM( INPUT )
```

will fail if there are no more input data remaining to be read. Furthermore, other statements may be transformed into *conditional statements* (i.e., statements that can fail) by the inclusion of one of the following relational operators within them:

Relational operator	Meaning
LT(i,j)	The integer (expression) i is less than the integer (expression) j.
GT(i,j)	i is greater than j.
EQ(i,j)	i is equal to j.
LE(i,j)	i is less than or equal to j.
GE(i,j)	i is greater than or equal to j.
NE(i,j)	i is not equal to j.
IDENT(s,t)	The string (expression) s is identical to the string (expression) t, character-for-character.
DIFFER(s,t)	s and t are not identical.

The statement that contains one of these will succeed or fail accordingly as the relation described above is true or false, for the current values of the arguments i and j (or s and t). For example,

```
I  =  LT( I,N )  I  +  1
```

has within it the relational operator LT(I , N) . If the value of the variable I is less than the value of N, then LT(I , N) is true and the statement succeeds. If LT(I , N) had not been true, then execution of the remainder of the statement would not take place. That is, the calculation I + 1 and assignment to I of the result would not be done. This is generally the case; whenever part of a statement fails, the remainder of the statement will *not* be executed.

Returning to the go to part of a statement, it can have any of the forms

: (label)
: S(label)
: F(label)
: S(label$_1$) F(label$_2$)

The first form is an *unconditional go to*; i.e., "label" is the label of the statement to which execution will transfer after the current statement, regardless of whether or not the current statement succeeds. The second form causes a transfer to the statement labeled "label," but only if the current statement succeeds. The third form is the converse of the second; the transfer takes place upon failure, rather than success, for the current statement. The fourth form combines the second and third, with "label$_1$" denoting the transfer for success and "label$_2$" denoting the transfer for failure.

To illustrate, consider the following SNOBOL program, which lists and counts a deck containing an unknown number of input data cards:

```
N  =  0
LOOP OUTPUT  =  INPUT  :F(EXIT)
     N  =  N  +  1  :(LOOP)
EXIT OUTPUT  =  'THE NUMBER OF CARDS LISTED  =  '  N
END
```

Here, the statement labeled LOOP is repeatedly executed until it fails, i.e., until there are no more input cards. At that time, control passes to the statement labeled EXIT, which prints the card count N, and the program terminates.

Program execution always terminates when control reaches the END statement. Furthermore, END can be designated within the go to part of *any* statement in the program. For instance, the following modification lists input records without printing the record count:

```
N  =  0
LOOP OUTPUT  =  INPUT  :F (END)
     N  =  N  +  1  :(LOOP)
END
```

Relational operators are often used in SNOBOL to control the *number of times* a series of statements is to be repeated. The following general scheme is commonly used for this purpose:

```
        I = 1
LOOP ┌─────────────────────────────────┐
     │ series of statements to be repeated │
     └─────────────────────────────────┘
        I = LT(I,N) I+1        :S(LOOP)
```

Here, LOOP labels the first statement in the series, and N denotes the number of times that the series is to be repeated. As long as I remains less than N, I will be incremented and control will transfer back to the beginning of the series.

3-5. Character String Manipulation: Pattern Matching and Conditional Assignment

SNOBOL's facilities for character string manipulation are extremely versatile. At the heart of these facilities are its pattern matching functions. A *pattern match* is the systematic examination of a particular string, known as the *subject string,* for an occurrence of one or more alternative strings, known collectively as the *pattern.* Whenever a pattern match is desired in the program, it is written either as a separate statement, in the form

subject pattern

or as part of an assignment statement, in the form

subject pattern = expression

In either case, the pattern match is said to *succeed* or *fail,* depending, respectively, on whether or not the subject string contains one of the strings described by the pattern. Thus, any such statement can have a go to part appended at its right end, and transfer from this statement can be conditioned to the success or failure of its pattern match. In the second (assignment) form above, the value of the expression on the right will be assigned to that part of the subject string for which the pattern match succeeds, and *only if* the match succeeds.

To illustrate these points, let us consider the *simplest* kind of pattern, the lone character string, such as 'ƀ'. (More complex forms of patterns are developed in later sections, after the basic process is understood.) Consider the variable S, which might have the value 'EACHƀPREPOSITION'. Then the pattern match below specifies the leftmost occurrence in S of 'ƀ':

S 'ƀ'

It will succeed or fail depending on whether or not 'ƀ' occurs in S. For the value of S given above, therefore, this pattern match will succeed. If we had written this pattern match as part of an assignment, such as

S 'ƀ' = '*'

we are literally saying, "replace the leftmost occurrence of 'ƀ' in S by '*', and do nothing if 'ƀ' does not occur in S." For the value of S given above, therefore, this statement would leave the value of S as 'EACH*PREPOSITION'.

The *subject* in a pattern match must be a variable name or array reference. The *pattern* itself, however, can be comprised of many parts, connected by operators and containing any one of a number of pattern matching functions. In the following sections, we begin to explore some of these operators and functions, and then put them to use in text processing applications.

3-5.1 Concatenation and Alternation

The principal operators that can be used within a pattern are concatenation ('ƀ') and alternation (|). In the pattern match

S T U

S is the subject and T U is the pattern. T and U are, individually, variables. This pattern match succeeds with the leftmost occurrence in S of the string that results from concatenating the value of T and the value of U. If S, T, and U have the values 'EACHƀPREPOSITION', 'P', and 'OS', respectively, then the match succeeds with the first occurrence in S of 'POS', which is circled below:

S | EACHƀPRE (POS) ITION

If, on the other hand, we had written

S T U = "

then the results would have been:

S | EACHƀPREITION

Alternation, on the other hand, denotes a series of two or more *alternatives* that can cause the pattern match to succeed. For example, if we write

S T | U

then the leftmost occurrence of T *or* U in S will cause the pattern match to succeed. When applied to the values shown above for S, T, and U, this match will succeed with the string that is circled below:

S | EACHƀ(P)REPOSITION

3-5.2   Other Pattern Matching Functions

In addition to concatenation and alternation, SNOBOL provides a collection of functions that, when used together, can describe quite powerful and intricate pattern matching operations. These functions are defined in the list below, and their use is illustrated in the following paragraphs. In these definitions, t denotes any string or string expression and i denotes any integer or integer expression.

Pattern matching function	String within the subject S for which the pattern match will succeed
ANY(t)	The leftmost occurrence in S of any one character that appears in t.
ARB	An *arb*itrary string in S, of any length (see below for more discussion of ARB).
BREAK(t)	All characters in S up to, but not including, the leftmost occurrence of some character within t.
LEN	An arbitrary string in S, of length i (see below for more discussion of LEN).
NOTANY(t)	The leftmost occurrence in S of a character that is *not any* of the characters that appear in t.
REM	The remainder, or right-hand end, of S (see below for more discussion of REM).
SPAN(t)	The leftmost occurrence of one or more characters in S up to, but not including, the next occurrence of some character that is *not* in t.

The functions ARB, LEN, and REM are illustrated in a subsequent section, after we present more of the dynamics of pattern matching. The other functions are illustrated below, assuming in each case that the subject string S has the value

S | EACHbPREPOSITIONbOPERATESbSYNTACTICALLYb. |

Pattern match	String in S for which the match succeeds
S ANY ('AEIOU')	The leftmost vowel in S, i.e., 'E'.
S NOTANY('AEIOU')	The leftmost nonvowel in S, i.e., 'C'.
S BREAK('b')	The string up to, but not including the leftmost 'b' i.e., 'EACH'
S SPAN('b')	The first string of blanks up to, but not including, the next nonblank, i.e., the string 'b'.
S SPAN('AEIOU')	All characters up to the first nonvowel, i.e., 'EA'

3-5.3   *Positioning and Composing Pattern Matching Functions*

The above examples indicate that, so far, pattern matching is somewhat "bogged down" at the left end of the subject string. This is not the case in general. Although the pattern match operation *always* proceeds from left to right in the subject string, the *number* of functions that comprise the *full* definition of a pattern can be more than one. Furthermore, the position in the subject string at which the pattern match takes place can also be controlled.

A pattern can be composed from two or more functions by using either the concatenation or the alternation operator. For instance, the pattern ANY('AEIOU') NOTANY('AEIOU') can be written to denote the leftmost occurrence in the subject string of a vowel followed by a consonant. For example, for the string S given above, the pattern match

```
S   ANY('AEIOU') NOTANY('AEIOU')
```

succeeds with the string 'AC' that appears in positions 2 and 3 of S. Similarly, the pattern match

```
S   SPAN('ƀ') BREAK('ƀ')
```

succeeds with the string 'ƀPREPOSITION' in positions 5-16 of S. Thus, we have isolated a single *word* out of a sentence. This will be useful in more ambitious programming problems shown in later sections.

Sometimes it is necessary to control the *position* within the subject string at which the pattern match must succeed. For example, suppose we have a string S in which we want to delete leading blanks. The pattern matching assignment

```
S   SPAN('ƀ')  =   "
```

will delete the first string of blanks in S, but these are not necessarily leading blanks. The following two examples illustrate the different effects of this statement with different values for S:

S	Effect on S of S SPAN('ƀ') = "
EACHƀPREPOSITIONƀƀƀ	EACHPREPOSITIONƀƀƀ
ƀƀƀEACHƀPREPOSITION	EACHƀPREPOSITION

To limit the pattern match operation to take place at a fixed position within the subject string, the POS and RPOS functions are available. To understand how these work, one must view each character in the subject string as occupying a fixed position, the first in position 0, the second in position 1, and so forth. There is also associated a so-called right position for each character, which designates its position relative to the right-hand end of the subject string. Right position 0 is occupied by the rightmost character, right position 1 by the next rightmost, and so forth. The following subject string is marked to show the position and right position for each of its characters:

$$ bbbEACHbPREPOSITION $$
$$ \text{position} \rightarrow 0\ 1\ 2\ 3\ 4\ 5\ 6\ 7\ 8\ 9 $$
$$ 9\ 8\ 7\ 6\ 5\ 4\ 3\ 2\ 1\ 0 \leftarrow \text{right position} $$

An appearance of the function POS(n) within a composite pattern designates that the *next successive* pattern match function to its right *begin* at position n of the subject string. The function RPOS(n) designates that the *immediately preceding* pattern match function on its left *terminate* at right position n of the subject string. For example, the assignment

S POS(0) SPAN('b') = "

will delete the longest string of *leading* blanks in S but no others. On the other hand, the assignment

S SPAN('b') RPOS(0) = "

will delete all *trailing* blanks in S, but no others.

The most general kinds of pattern matching functions are ARB, LEN, and REM. They are general in the sense that they will succeed regardless of the content of the subject string. They are always used in composition with one of the POS, RPOS, or other functions discussed above.

The ARB function succeeds with an arbitrary string of any length. When used within a pattern, ARB serves to "bridge" a portion of the subject string that appears between two strictly defined patterns. For instance, the pattern match

S 'b' ARB '.'

succeeds with the leftmost occurrence of *any* string that begins with 'b' and ends with '.'.

The LEN function is written as LEN(i), where i is an integer-valued expression denoting the length of the string that will cause the pattern match to succeed. For instance,

S 'b' LEN(3) '.'

will succeed only if there is a blank in S that is followed by a string of length 3 (but with arbitrary characters) and then a '.'. LEN, then, is slightly more restrictive than ARB in its requirement for success.

The function REM succeeds with any string that is the *remainder* of S, and is usually preceded by either a POS function or some other function that identifies a pattern in the initial part of S. For example, the pattern match and assignment

```
S  BREAK('ƀ')  SPAN('ƀ')  '.'  REM  =  "
```

deletes from S the last word in a sentence, the period `'.'`, and whatever follows the period. If S is initially

S | SOMEƀAREƀHEREƀ.ƀBUTƀNOTƀALLƀ |

then this assignment will leave S as follows:

S | SOMEƀAREƀ |

3-5.4 *Immediate and Conditional Assignment*

During the process of a pattern match operation, it is often useful to extract matched portions from the subject string and store them in other locations. For example, when the pattern match

```
S  BREAK('ƀ')
```

is executed, it will succeed with the leftmost string in S that is followed by a blank, i.e., the leftmost *word* in S.

In order to assign this word as the value of another variable, say T, either of the following operators may be used:

Operator	Meaning of S P $ T
$	*Immediate* assignment of the matched part of S (for the pattern P) to the variable T. If the match does not succeed, " will be assigned to T.
	Conditional assignment of the matched part of S to T. If the match does not succeed, no assignment will be made, and T will retain its previous value.

To illustrate, consider the subject string S whose value is `'EACHƀPREPOSITIONƀOPERATESƀSYNTACTICALLYƀ.'` and the following statements:

Statement	Resulting value of T
S BREAK('ƀ') $ T	'EACH'
S BREAK('ƀ') . T	'EACH'
S SPAN('ƀ') BREAK('ƀ') $ T	'PREPOSITION'
S 'ƀƀ' . T	(no assignment is made)

3-5.5 Precedence of Operators

The pattern matching operators are applied from left to right in the subject string. The assignment operators have *higher* precedence than concatenation and alternation. This means that in a pattern match of the form

S T U . V or S T U $ V

the assignment to V will be the pattern matched by U, and not the pattern matched by T U. In order to override this precedence, parentheses can be used. For instance, S (T U) . V indicates that the pattern matched by T U will be assigned to V. Suppose that S has the value 'EACHbPREPOSITION'. Then the following pattern matching assignments illustrate these characteristics of precedence:

Pattern match	String in S causing the match to succeed	Result assigned to V
S SPAN('b) BREAK('b') . V	'bPREPOSITION'	'PREPOSITION'
S (SPAN('b') BREAK('b')) . V	'bPREPOSITION'	'bPREPOSITION'
S ANY('AEIOU') ARB . V 'b'	'EACHb'	'ACH'

The third example shows that the assignment operation may appear anywhere within a pattern and not necessarily at its right end. In this case, the first string in S that follows a vowel and precedes a 'b' will be assigned to V.

3-5.6 Pattern Assignment and Some Useful Patterns

Sometimes the same pattern match will be needed in several different parts of a program, and the pattern itself is long and tedious to write. To avoid rewriting the same pattern each time that it is needed, SNOBOL provides the capability to assign the *pattern itself* to a distinct simple variable, and then name the variable each time that the pattern match is needed.

To illustrate, suppose that we want to use the pattern

'bAb' | 'bANb' | 'bTHEb'

to denote the selection within S of an article "a," "an," or "the." Then we can write the following pattern definition at the start of the program:

ART = 'bAb' | 'bANb' | 'bTHEb'

Now, whenever we want to search a subject string S for an article, and assign that article to another variable, say WORD, then we could write

```
S   ART . WORD
```

rather than

```
S   ('ƀAƀ' | 'ƀANƀ' | 'ƀTHEƀ') . WORD
```

The following are useful patterns for detecting and isolating some basic elements from free-running text:

Pattern (P)	Meaning of the match S P
NOTANY('ƀ')	The leftmost nonblank (i.e., the beginning of a word) in S.
BREAK('ƀ')	The leftmost word in S.
POS(I) ARB 'ƀ' BREAK('ƀ') . V	V will contain the next complete word *after* position I in S.
P = 'ING' | 'ED' | 'S' (SPAN('ƀ') | '') (ARB P) . V 'ƀ'	V will contain the leftmost word in S that ends with ING, ED, or S. Here, SPAN('ƀ') | '' denotes the first series of *zero* or more blanks.
BREAK('ƀ') . V (SPAN('ƀ') | '') RPOS(0)	V will contain the *rightmost* word in S.
PUNC = 'ƀ.ƀ' | 'ƀ?ƀ' | 'ƀ!ƀ' (ARB PUNC) . V	V will contain the leftmost *sentence* within S, including its final punctuation (., ?, or !).

3-5.7 *Intermediate Assignment of Position within a Pattern Match*

It is often useful to maintain, as a separate variable, the *location* within the subject string at which a pattern match succeeds. For instance, if we are searching for each word in S, one after the other, the position where one word ends will tell us where to begin the search for the next word. The present location of a pattern match is given by the unary prefix operator @. When written before a variable, as in

```
@ I
```

this operator designates intermediate assignment to I of the current position in the subject string of the pattern match.

Suppose, for example, that the subject S contains the value 'EACHƀPREPOSITIONƀOPERATESƀSYNTACTICALLYƀ.' and we want to isolate each word in succession, assigning it to the array WORDS, which might be defined as follows:

```
WORDS = ARRAY <50>
```

Then if we initialize I = 0, the pattern match

```
S   POS(I) BREAK('ƀ') . WORDS <1> @ I
```

will isolate the first word in S and assign it to the first entry in WORDS, or WORDS<1>. Furthermore, it will leave in I the position in S that follows the last character of that word. Thus, repetition of this statement will successively place each word of S in WORDS<1>. Now, to put these words in different locations of WORDS, we let J increment for each repetition of this statement, as follows:

```
        I = 0
        J = 1
LOOP    S POS(I) BREAK('ƀ') . WORDS<J> @ -I  :F(OUT)
        J = LT(I,SIZE(S)) J+1     :S(LOOP)
OUT
```

This loop will be continued until either S contains no more words (denoted by :F(OUT)) or I is no longer less than the size of S. The result of execution for S = 'EACHƀPREPOSITIONƀOPERATESƀSYNTACTICALLYƀ.' is

WORDS

Unassigned
Entries in
WORDS

3-6 Built-In and Programmer-Defined Functions
for String Manipulation

All of the pattern matching functions presented in the previous section are useful for the purpose of string *manipulation* as well as string *analysis*. That is, any pattern matching statement of the form

S P

can be extended to an assignment statement of the form

S P = T

This will cause not only a pattern match to be performed with subject S and pattern P, but also an assignment of T to replace that part of S which matches P. Compare, for example, the pattern matching statement

```
S  BREAK('ƀ')  .  WORD
```

with the assignment statement

```
S  BREAK('ƀ')  .  WORD  =  "
```

In the second statement, the first word in S is assigned to WORD *and* is deleted from S.

Often the built-in functions are not sufficient to suit the particular needs of a programming problem. SNOBOL provides facilities by which the programmer can extend this functional repertoire by defining new functions and invoking them in the usual way. For example, suppose we want to define a function named REVERSE which will, when invoked, reverse the characters in an arbitrary string X. For example, if X = 'EACH', then the statement B = REVERSE(X) will leave B = 'HCAE'.

To define a function, we must first write a DEFINE *statement* at the top of the program. Its general form is

```
DEFINE ('name(parameters)locals')
```

Here, "name" identifies the function, "parameters" lists the different parameters of the function, and "locals" identifies the variables that are to be considered as local to the function. The meaning of these different notions will be made clear in the example below.

The second step in defining a function is to write SNOBOL statements that describe what the function will do when it is invoked. These statements are usually placed at the end of a SNOBOL program (just before the END statement) and begin with a statement whose label is the function name itself. For instance, consider the process of reversing an arbitrary string S, by way of a function named REVERSE:

```
REVERSE  I  =  0
         J  =  SIZE(S)
RV1      I  =  GT(J,I+1)  I+1    :F(RETURN)
         S LEN(1) . T POS(I) ARB . U LEN(1) . V
         POS(J)  =  V U T
         J  =  J-1           :(RV1)
```

This series of statements will appear at the end of the program. We note three different kinds of entities herein: the "parameter" S, the "local variables" I, J, T, U, and V, and the undefined statement label RETURN.

The parameters in a function (S in this case) should not be mistaken as variables. Although they play the same role as variable names in the description of the function, parameters have no values. The parameters are always replaced by actual variable names or values at the time the function is invoked. For example, if we invoke the REVERSE function by saying

```
B = REVERSE ('EACH')
```

then the parameter S is replaced by the value 'EACH' whenever it occurs among the statements that describe REVERSE.

The variables I, J, T, U, and V in the description of REVERSE are "local" in the sense that the values they assume during execution of the statements that describe the function are not accessible from other statements in the program itself. Moreover, the program may define other variables named I, J, T, U, and/or V with the assurance that their values will not be affected by an invocation of REVERSE.

Finally, the statement label RETURN that appears in the description of RE-VERSE indicates that execution should "return" to the statement from which the function was originally invoked.

Thus the function description is a sequence of statements that can be invoked from any one or more different statements of the main program, each time with a different variable name or value (called an *argument*) to which the function should be applied. When finished, execution of the function returns control to that point in the program immediately following the invocation. Consider the following complete program:

```
                RWORDS = ARRAY<100>
                DEFINE ('REVERSE(S)I,J,T,U,V')
LOOP1           S = INPUT          :F(END)
                I = 0
                J = 1
LOOP2           S POS(I) BREAK('ƀ') . X @ I :F(OUT)
                RWORDS<J> = REVERSE(X)
                J = LT(I, SIZE(S)) J+1  :S(LOOP2)
OUT             I = 1
OUT1            OUTPUT = RWORDS(I)
                I = LT(I,J) I+1  :S(OUT1)F(LOOP1)
REVERSE         I = 0
                J = SIZE(S)
RV1             I = GT(J,I+1) I+1  :F(RETURN)
                S LEN(1) . T POS(I) ARB . LEN(1) . V
                  POS(J) = V U T
                J = J-1    :(RV1)
END
EACH PREPOSITION OPERATES SYNTACTICALLY .
```

The reader should see that this program reads one card at a time, separates its individual words, reverses them, and then prints the reversed words in a list.

Also it should be clear that the variables named I and J in the main program are totally unrelated to the (local) variables with the same names in the description of the function REVERSE. Let us trace the activity of the function REVERSE when it is first invoked by the statement

RWORDS<J> = REVERSE(X)

where X has the value 'EACH'.

Here, each occurrence of the parameter S in the description of REVERSE is replaced by the argument X. Now, execution of REVERSE yields the following sequence of values for locals I, J, T, U, and V, and the argument X from the calling program:

X	'EACH'	'HACE'	'HCAE'
I	0 1	2	
J	4	3	2
T	'E'	'A'	
U	'AC'	''	
V	'H'	'C'	

The sequence of values each variable takes on is shown from left to right. As shown, the first and last characters are exchanged in X, then the second and next to last, and so forth. I points to the first character and moves to the right (in the positive direction), and J simultaneously moves in the negative direction from the last character. When they meet in the middle of X (i.e., GT(J, I + 1) is no longer true), the reversal is complete, and control RETURNs to the invocation.

Whenever a function is defined, there must be provision to RETURN control to the invocation. On the other hand, a function can be invoked from the main program as many times as it is needed. Furthermore, functions may contain invocations of other functions within them.

3-7   Hints for Diagnosing Errors in SNOBOL Programs: Program Trace

The intricacies of pattern matching and string manipulation provide many opportunities for errors in SNOBOL programming. SNOBOL provides the TRACE built-in function to aid the programmer in diagnosing program errors. During program execution, any or all of the following values may be automatically displayed using TRACE:

(1) the value of a given variable each time that its value is reassigned.
(2) the name of a function each time that it is invoked.
(3) the label of a program statement each time the statement is executed.

These actions are invoked, respectively, by each of the following:

```
TRACE('I','VALUE')
TRACE('F','FUNCTION')
TRACE('L','LABEL')
```

In the first, the variable named I will have its value printed each time it is assigned. In the second, the function named F will be printed each time it is invoked. In the third, the statement label L will be printed each time its associated statement is executed.

In order for these statements to be effective, the special "system variable" named &TRACE should be initialized at some positive integer value, say 100. For example,

```
&TRACE = 100
```

means that up to 100 lines of tracing information will be displayed (by way of TRACE function invocations) during execution of the program. Without this statement, the variable &TRACE will be set (by default) to the value 0, so that no tracing information will be printed.

Questions and Exercises

1. Write a two-statement SNOBOL program that will read and list the contents of a deck of input cards. Test the program by providing as input data a copy of the program itself, and verify that it lists itself.

2. Write another SNOBOL program that will list and count a deck of cards, bypassing all cards in the deck that are blank. The number of cards listed and counted should be printed below the last card.

3. A common text processing application is the generation of frequency counts for different classes of words and other tokens in a running text. Write a SNOBOL program that counts the number of occurrences of each of the following classes of tokens:

   (i) articles 'A', 'AN', and 'THE'
   (ii) sentence delimiters '.', '?', and '!'
   (iii) other punctuation marks ':', ';', '(', ')', '.', and '–'.

   Your program should use a three-element array, where each element counts the number of occurrences of each class. The output should look like

```
CLASS                      FREQUENCY COUNT
ARTICLES                         27
SENTENCES                         9
OTHER PUNCTUATION                11
```

The numbers in the right-hand columns are those that will have been developed in the array. Your program can assume that no sentence is divided between two input cards, no card contains more than one sentence, and that each punctuation mark is preceded and followed by a blank space.

4. To identify whether or not a word has a particular ending, the RPOS (0) function can be used. This forces the pattern match to succeed at the right end of the word. For instance, if the variable WORD has the value ' EX– CEEDED ' then the pattern match

```
WORD  'ED'
```

will succeed with the first instance of ED in WORD , as circled below:

EXCE (ED) ED

However, the pattern match

```
WORD  'ED'  RPOS(0)
```

will succeed for the ED that appears on the right end of WORD , as circled below:

EXCE ED (ED)

Using this fact, write patterns that will succeed for each of the following situations:

(a)   WORD ends with S, ED, or ING.
(b)   WORD begins with DE and ends with ED.
(c)   WORD contains DE and ED (but in either order).

5. Write SNOBOL statements that will read a text from input cards and print it. In this case, the program should allow for a word to be split between two adjacent cards, but should not split such a word between two lines of output. For example, if the input is

```
  SITION OPERATES SYNTACTICALLY.
        EACH PREPO
```

then the output should be

```
                          EACH
PREPOSITION OPERATES SYNTACTICALLY  .
```

The program should permit any number of input cards, and should assume that no word exceeds 30 characters in length.

6. Refine the above program by forcing the first word of each printed line to begin in position 1, even though its corresponding input card may not. The example above, for instance, should be printed as

```
EACH
PREPOSITION OPERATES SYNTACTICALLY  .
```

7. Write a program that will identify all the different tokens in a text that are not ordinary words (i.e., punctuation marks, numerals, formulas, abbreviations, and so forth), and list them without repetition. You may assume that there are no more than 100 such tokens in the text. For example, if the following text is input

```
THE TEMPERATURE WAS 72 , A GALE-FORCE WIND BLEW , AND
OVER 100 PERSONS BEGAN TO FILE OUT
```

then the output will be

```
72
,
100
.
```

Here, you should define as an ordinary word any sequence of nonblank characters composed entirely of letters (A–Z) and hyphens (-), but only if the hyphens are properly embedded within the sequence. Note that only one occurrence of each nonordinary word is listed. [*Hint:* For each nonordinary word encountered, add it to an array, but only if it is not already there. Also keep a count of the number of such words that are already in the array throughout the process.]

8. Write a SNOBOL function named PLURAL that will convert any given noun to its plural form, according to the following rule:

(a) If the noun ends in Y, change the ending to IES.
(b) If the noun ends in two consonants, add ES.
(c) Otherwise, add S.

9. Show the effects (strengths and weaknesses) of the above rules by writing a program that reads the following words and prints each one together with its plural form (as derived by PLURAL):

```
FOLLY       FOX
KISS        BUS
PUN         MITT
PUNCH       RELAY
```

10. From your experience with question 9, refine the rules of question 8 and the function PLURAL so that it generates correct plurals for a wider variety of cases.

11. Often an occurrence of a word in a text can have two or more different meanings, depending upon the context in which it is used. It is important for programs that try to "understand" language to disambiguate such words when they occur in a text. For example, if the word A occurs in an English text, it is generally an article and part of a noun phrase. However, when A occurs at the beginning of a new line and is followed by a period, it serves instead as a marginal heading.

Write a SNOBOL program that disambiguates each occurrence of the word A and follows it with either #ARTICLE# or #HEADING# while printing the entire text. For example, if the following input occurs,

```
A LIST WILL BE A FOOT LONG , AND CONTAIN THE ITEMS
BELOW :
           A .   A BALLOON STRING
           B .   A BUBBLE
           C .   A HAIR FROM A HORSE
```

the output should appear as

```
A #ARTICLE# LIST WILL BE A #ARTICLE# FOOT LONG, AND
CONTAIN THE ITEMS BELOW :
       A  #HEADING#  .  A  #ARTICLE# BALLOON STRING
       B  .  A  #ARTICLE# BUBBLE
       C  .  A  #ARTICLE# HAIR FROM A #ARTICLE# HORSE
```

12. (Difficult program) Write a SNOBOL program that will read an input text and print it so that each line is left- and right-margin adjusted. That is, each line should begin and end with a nonblank character. No word should be split between lines, even though a word may be broken between input cards (see question 5 above). The program should "fill out" each line by systematically adding blank spaces between words in the line. Each line should be exactly 60 characters wide.

13. Briefly compare PL/I with SNOBOL by selecting one of your PL/I programs and rewriting it in SNOBOL. Similarly, select one of your SNOBOL programs and rewrite it in PL/I. What conclusions can you draw about the relative strengths and weaknesses of the two languages for text processing from this particular experience?

Chapter 4

Overview of Text Processing Packages and Applications

In Chapters 2 and 3, we saw how two programming languages, PL/I and SNO-BOL, can be used for text processing. Each has relative strengths and weaknesses in different aspects of text processing. Yet, neither is as easy to use as the so-called text processing packages. These are designed principally for use by non-programmers. They are well-suited to a variety of common text processing tasks.

The four text processing packages that we present and illustrate in this chapter are KWIC, FAMULUS, the CMS Editor, and SCRIPT. These are only a small sample of the large number of text processing packages that are in use today. In Section 4-1 we illustrate how KWIC can be used for concordance generation. Section 4-2 presents FAMULUS and shows how it can be used in bibliographic information retrieval. Section 4-3 presents the essential aspects of the CMS Editor and shows its use in interactive text editing. Section 4-4 presents and illustrates the use of SCRIPT for automatic text formatting.

4-1 KWIC for Concordance Generation

A *concordance* is an alphabetical list of the words in a text, each with its surrounding context. A KWIC (*key word in context*) program is simply one that that can generate a concordance for any running text. Most computer installations have their own KWIC programs, and different programs have different selections of options that can be used for generating special concordances. For example, it may be useful in a given language analysis application to produce a concord-ance that contains only the occurrences of A, AN, and THE and their respective contexts. Another option may be to alphabetize the words reversed (i.e., in mirror-image form, such as GNIMROF in place of FORMING). This allows all words with the same ending (e.g., ING) to occur together.

Concordances are an extremely useful aid in text processing applications. For example, they are helpful in determining the various uses of a particular word or phrase, since all occurrences of the word or phrase appear clustered together in the concordance. Concordances can also be used as an aid to developing indexes from titles in a bibliography.

A brief look at the programming aspects of concordance generation reveals that the following programming tasks are needed:

(1)   extracting the words and their contexts from the text to form a new file,
(2)   sorting that file of words into alphabetical order,
(3)   printing the alphabetized file.

This in itself is a fair programming effort. Furthermore, most concordance-generation programs provide other options, like printing only the occurrences of a preselected list of words, excluding occurrences of such words, or printing only one occurrence of each word together with the integer number of times that it occurs. Programming these options can require significant additional effort.

Because of the wide usefulness of concordances and because of the effort that would be required to write the concordance program, several different concordance-generating packaged programs have been developed and have become widely available. Some of these are quite general and transferable among different computers. Others are very limited in their capabilities and are not designed for distribution.

4-1.1   Sample Concordance

As an example, Fig. 4-1 shows part of a concordance that was generated from the sample text given in Chapter 1 (Fig. 1-2).

4-1.2   Text Record Layout and Control Cards

In order to generate a concordance using the KWIC program, two basic requirements must be fulfilled:

(1)   the text must be in a form suitable for the KWIC program,

(2)   *control cards* must be prepared, which define the particular form of the text and the options that are requested for the concordance.

Figure 4-2 shows the text that was prepared for input to the KWIC program. It is encoded into a series of 80-character records, with the first 71 characters containing text and the next 9 characters containing a record identification code.

```
E, OFFICE SPACE, ETC., EQUIPMENT,        PLANT FACILITIES AND OFFICE FURNITUR   SAM00110
ADE . THE R&D PROGRAMS HAVE HAD A         PROFOUNDR&D PROGRAMS OF THE LAST DEC   SAM00040
RAMS OF THE LAST DECADE . THE R&D         PROGRAMS HAVE HAD A PROFOUNDR&D PROG   SAM00040
&D PROGRAMS HAVE HAD A PROFOUNDR&D        PROGRAMS OF THE LAST DECADE . THE R    SAM00040
, EFFECT ON ECONOMIC GROWTH AND           PROSPERITY IN THE COMMUNITY , STATE    SAM00050
INERY AND        2.  BUSINESS             PROSPERITY, THROUGH PURCHASE OF MACH   SAM00010
      2.  BUSINESS PROSPERITY, THROUGH    PURCHASE OF MACHINERY AND              SAM00010
PROGRAMS OF THE LAST DECADE .  THE        R&D PROGRAMS HAVE HAD A PROFOUNDR&D     SAM00040
HE R&D PROGRAMS HAVE HAD A PROFOUND        REGION .  AT EVERY GEOGRAPHIC LEVEL    SAM00040
THESE ACTIVITIES BENEFIT .       AND      REGION HAS DIFFERENT NEEDS AND         SAM00060
      EACH COMMUNITY . STATE , AND        RESEARCH AND DEVELOPMENT               SAM00140
THE GEOGRAPHICAL DISTRIBUTION OF          RESOURCES -- MANPOWER , EQUIPMENT ,    SAM00010
   LEADERSHIP -- TO MEET DIFFERENT        S JOBS  ALIGNMENT BETWEEN OF TRAININ   SAM00150
G AND THE SKILLS DEMANDED IN TODAY'       SATISFY NATIONAL NEEDS MUST OFTEN FO   SAM00130
CUS AN A VARIETY OF APPLICATIONS TO       SCALE NATIONWIDE JUST BEGINNING TO U   SAM00170
NDERSTAND THE FULL IMPACT OF LARGE        SCIENCE AND ENGINEERING , WITH         SAM00030
   TECHNICAL JOBS IN THE AREAS OF         SCIENCE AND THECHNOLOGY TO    THESE    SAM00080
NEEDS .  EFFECTIVE APPLICATION OF         SKILLS DEMANDED IN TODAY'S JOBS  ALI   SAM00160
GNMENT BETWEEN OF TRAINING AND THE        SOURCE OF INCREASING INTEREST AND CO   SAM00130
NCEFN . WE ARE   ACTIVITIES IS A          SPACE, ETC.,  EQUIPMENT, PLANT FACIL   SAM00030
ITIES AND OFFICE FURNITURE, OFFICE        SPECIFIC LOCAL NEEDS.        THE C     SAM00110
OMPONENTS OF NATIONAL NEEDS, I.E.,        STATE ,     EFFECT ON ECONOMIC GROWTH  SAM00180
AND PROSPERITY IN THE COMMUNITY ,         STATE , AND REGION HAS DIFFERENT NEE   SAM00050
DS AND         EACH COMMUNITY ,           SUPPORTING PERSONNEL .                 SAM00140
                                                                                 SAM00090
CE AND ENGINEERING , WITH                 TECHNICAL JOBS IN THE AREAS OF  SCIEN   SAM00080
```

Fig. 4-1. Part of a concordance.

```
THE  GEOGRAPHICAL   DISTRIBUTION OF RESEARCH AND DEVELOPMENT        SAM00010
ACTIVITIES IS A   SOURCE  OF INCREASING INTEREST AND CONCERN .  WE ARE      SAM00030
JUST BEGINNING TO UNDERSTAND THE FULL IMPACT OF LARGE SCALE NATIONWIDE SAM00030
R&D PROGRAMS OF THE LAST DECADE .   THE R&D PROGRAMS HAVE HAD A PROFOUNDSAM00040
EFFECT ON ECONOMIC GROWTH AND PROSPERITY IN THE COMMUNITY , STATE ,    SAM00050
AND REGION .  AT EVERY GEOGRAPHIC LEVEL THESE ACTIVITIES BENEFIT .     SAM00060
1. EMPLOYMENT, THROUGH MORE JOBS AND ESPECIALLY THROUGH MORE     SAM00070
TECHNICAL JOBS IN THE AREAS OF SCIENCE AND ENGINEERING , WITH    SAM00080
SUPPORTING PERSONNEL .                                           SAM00090
2.  BUSINESS PROSPERITY, THROUGH PURCHASE OF MACHINERY AND       SAM00010
EQUIPMENT, PLANT FACILITIES AND OFFICE FURNITURE, OFFICE SPACE, ETC.,  SAM00115
AND                                                              SAM00115
3.  EDUCATION , THROUGH MODERNIZATION CURRICULA AND A CLOSER     SAM00120
ALIGNMENT BETWEEN OF TRAINING AND THE SKILLS DEMANDED IN TODAY'S JOBS  SAM00130
                                                                 SAM00135
EACH COMMUNITY , STATE , AND REGION HAS DIFFERENT NEEDS AND      SAM00140
DIFFERENT RESOURCES — MANPOWER , EQUIPMENT , LEADERSHIP — TO MEET    SAM00150
THESE NEEDS .  EFFECTIVE APPLICATION OF SCIENCE AND THECHNOLOGY TO   SAM00160
SATISFY NATIONAL NEEDS MUST OFTEN FOCUS AN A VARIETY OF APPLICATIONS TOSAM00170
THE COMPONENTS OF NATIONAL NEEDS, I.E., SPECIFIC LOCAL NEEDS .   SAM00180
```

Fig. 4-2. Input text for concordance.

As shown here, a word may not be continued from one record to another when it will not fit entirely at the end of one record.

The control cards that are required to run the KWIC program serve to define for the program the record length, the text length, and any other options that may be requested for the run. (Some of these options are illustrated in Section 4-1.3.) Figure 4-3 shows the control cards that were used to generate the concordance in Fig. 4-1 from the input in Fig. 4-2.

```
CONCORDANCE FOR SAMPLE TEXT
RECLNG=80
TXTLNG=71
IDPOS=72
IDLNG=9
```

Fig. 4-3. Control cards for concordance generation.

4-1.3   *Included and Excluded Words*

Perhaps the most useful option in concordance generation is the ability to specify either:

(1)   that only certain words be included in the concordance listing, or
(2)   that certain words be excluded from the concordance.

Inclusion of selected words is useful when one wants to analyze limited classes (such as articles A, AN, and THE) without being encumbered by a large, bulky concordance that results from including all other words as well. *Exclusion* of certain words is useful in reducing the bulk of the concordance by omitting frequently occurring words and other tokens (such as punctuation marks). Figure 4-4 shows the partial concordance that results from including only the words A, AN, and THE in the sample text.

4-1.4   *Other Options*

In addition to word exclusion and inclusion, the concordance program may have the ability to order the words alphabetically from right to left. That is, all words with the same ending will occur together. An example is given in Fig. 4-5, which shows a partial concordance with reversed ordering from the sample text. This kind of concordance is sometimes called a *reverse KWIC*.

4-1.5   *Deck Setup for Running KWIC*

To run the KWIC program on an IBM machine, a specific set of control cards is needed. These are shown in Fig. 4-6. The reader is advised that the particular information on these control cards is specific to the computer installation on which the KWIC program was run, and is generally not effective at other installations. A similar collection of control information would be required for running a KWIC program at any other installation.

```
CONCERN .  WE ARE     ACTIVITIES IS   A   SOURCE OF INCREASING INTEREST AND   SAM00030
HROUGH MODERNIZATION CURRICULA AND    A   CLOSER          3.    EDUCATION , T   SAM00120
ECADE .   THE R&D PROGRAMS HAVE HAD   A   PROFOUNDR&D PROGRAMS OF THE LAST D    SAM00040
NATIONAL NEEDS MUST OFTEN FOCUS AN    A   VARIETY OF APPLICATIONS TOSATISFY     SAM00170
FY NATIONAL NEEDS MUST OFTEN FOCUS    AN  A VARIETY OF APPLICATIONS TOSATIS     SAM00170
ESEARCH AND DEVELOPMENT               THE GEOGRAPHICAL DISTRIBUTION OF R        SAM00010
, WITH       TECHNICAL JOBS IN        THE AREAS OF SCIENCE AND ENGINEERING      SAM00080
ECONOMIC GROWTH AND PROSPERITY IN     THE COMMUNITY , STATE ,    EFFECT ON      SAM00050
E., SPECIFIC LOCAL NEEDS.             THE COMPONENTS OF NATIONAL NEEDS, I.      SAM00180
NWIDE JUST BEGINNING TO UNDERSTAND    THE FULL IMPACT OF LARGE SCALE NATIO      SAM00030
HAVE HAD A PROFOUNDR&D PROGRAMS OF    THE LAST DECADE .  THE R&D PROGRAMS       SAM00040
R&D PROGRAMS OF THE LAST DECADE .     THE R&D PROGRAMS HAVE HAD A PROFOUND      SAM00040
ALIGNMENT BETWEEN OF TRAINING AND     THE SKILLS DEMANDED IN TODAY'S JOBS       SAM00130
```

Fig. 4-4. Partial concordance with included words.

```
CURRICULA AND A CLOSER ALIGNMENT BETWEEN    OF TRAINING      AND THE SKILLS DEMANDED IN TODAY'S JOBS . EACH      SAM00130
OF INCREASING INTEREST AND CONCERN . WE ARE JUST BEGINNING   TO UNDERSTAND THE FULL IMPACT OF LARGE SCALE        SAM00030
MORE TECHNICAL JOBS IN THE AREAS OF SCIENCE AND ENGINEERING  , WITH SUPPORTING PERSONNEL . 2. BUSINESS          SAM00080
AND DEVELOPMENT ACTIVITIES IS A SOURCE OF INCREASING         INTEREST AND CONCERN . WE ARE JUST BEGINNING       SAM00020
IN THE AREAS OF SCIENCE AND ENGINEERING , WITH SUPPORTING    PERSONNEL . 2. BUSINESS PROSPERITY, THROUGH        SAM00080
OF TRAINING AND THE SKILLS DEMANDED IN TODAY'S JOBS . EACH   COMMUNITY , STATE , AND REGION HAS DIFFERENT       SAM00140
THE GEOGRAPHICAL DISTRIBUTION OF RESEARCH                    AND DEVELOPMENT ACTIVITIES IS A SOURCE OF          SAM00010
LEVEL THESE ACTIVITIES BENEFIT . 1. EMPLOYMENT, THROUGH      MORE JOBS AND ESPECIALLY THROUGH MORE              SAM00070
. 1. EMPLOYMENT, THROUGH MORE JOBS AND ESPECIALLY THROUGH    MORE TECHNICAL JOBS IN THE AREAS OF SCIENCE        SAM00070
WITH SUPPORTING PERSONNEL . 2. BUSINESS PROSPERITY, THROUGH  PURCHASE OF MACHINERY AND EQUIPMENT, PLANT         SAM00100
FURNITURE, OFFICE SPACE, ETC., AND 3. EDUCATION , THROUGH    MODERNIZATION CURRICULA AND A CLOSER ALIGNMENT     SAM00120
JOBS IN THE AREAS OF SCIENCE AND ENGINEERING , WITH          SUPPORTING PERSONNEL . 2. BUSINESS PROSPERITY,     SAM00080
R&D PROGRAMS HAVE HAD A PROFOUND EFFECT ON ECONOMIC GROWTH   AND PROSPERITY IN THE COMMUNITY , STATE , AND      SAM00050
                                      THE GEOGRAPHICAL       DISTRIBUTION OF RESEARCH AND DEVELOPMENT           SAM00010
THROUGH MORE JOBS AND ESPECIALLY THROUGH MORE TECHNICAL      JOBS IN THE AREAS OF SCIENCE AND ENGINEERING ,     SAM00080
TO THE COMPONENTS OF NATIONAL NEEDS, I.E., SPECIFIC LOCAL    NEEDS.                                             SAM00180
APPLICATION OF SCIENCE AND THECHNOLOGY TO SATISFY NATIONAL   NEEDS, MUST OFTEN FOCUS AN A VARIETY OF            SAM00170
AN A VARIETY OF APPLICATIONS TO THE COMPONENTS OF NATIONAL   NEEDS, I.E., SPECIFIC LOCAL NEEDS.                 SAM00180
AREAS OF SCIENCE AND ENGINEERING , WITH SUPPORTING PERSONNEL . 2. BUSINESS PROSPERITY, THROUGH PURCHASE OF     SAM00090
COMMUNITY , STATE , AND REGION . AT EVERY GEOGRAPHIC LEVEL   THESE ACTIVITIES BENEFIT . 1. EMPLOYMENT,          SAM00060
AND CONCERN . WE ARE JUST BEGINNING TO UNDERSTAND THE FULL   IMPACT OF LARGE SCALE NATIONWIDE R&D PROGRAMS      SAM00030
THECHNOLOGY TO SATISFY NATIONAL NEEDS MUST OFTEN FOCUS AN    A VARIETY OF APPLICATIONS TO THE COMPONENTS OF     SAM00170
MODERNIZATION CURRICULA AND A CLOSER ALIGNMENT BETWEEN       OF TRAINING AND THE SKILLS DEMANDED IN TODAY'S     SAM00130
SCIENCE AND THECHNOLOGY TO SATISFY NATIONAL NEEDS MUST OFTEN FOCUS AN A VARIETY OF APPLICATIONS TO THE          SAM00170
```

Fig. 4-5. Partial concordance with reversed ordering.

112

```
//TERMCONC  JOB  (0060,7022),TUCKER,CLASS=A,TIME=2

//  EXEC  GUKWIC

//GO.SYSIN  DD  *

//
```

Fig. 4-6. Deck setup for concordance generation.

4-2   FAMULUS for Bibliographic Information Retrieval

FAMULUS is a collection of programs that allow maintenance of bibliographic data on a computer in such a way that selected entries may be conveniently retrieved. FAMULUS originated in 1969 at the Pacific Southwest Forest and Range Experiment Station in Berkeley, California. The version that is illustrated in this section was made available in 1972 by the University College London Computer Centre.

FAMULUS allows one to store an entire bibliography on cards, tape, or disk; to add, delete, and alter individual entries; and to selectively retrieve information from the bibliography during normal research activity. Associated functions that support these tasks are the automatic sorting of entries into alphabetical order, automatic indexing, and searching the bibliography to find entries that satisfy given search criteria. Additional functions, such as statistical counts of words and word classes, encourage the use of FAMULUS as a tool in linguistic analysis.

4-2.1   Sample FAMULUS File and Printed Results

To illustrate the use of FAMULUS, we have encoded a portion of the References from the end of the book. We then created a "FAMULUS file" out of the bibliography's entries. A listing of the first five entries in that file is shown in Fig. 4-7.

The listing shown in Fig. 4-7 was generated using the FAMULUS program named GALLEY. The file itself was prepared on a terminal as a sequence of 80-character records using the CMS Editor (see Section 4-3). The GALLEY program was invoked, and this listing was obtained by way of the control cards shown below:

```
/ID/TEXT PROCESSING BIBLIOGRAPHY
/FIELDS/(AU,TI,PUB,DATE)
/PRINT BY SUBJECTS/
/SELECT/(1-5)
/NEW ID/T.P. BIBLIOGRAPHY - 1ST 5 ITEMS
```

T. P. BIBLIOGRAPHY – 1ST 5 ITEMS

ALLC BULLETIN ASOCIATION FOR LITERARY AND LINGUISTIC COMPUTING 1973–

AMERICAN JOURNAL OF COMPUTATIONAL LINGUISTICS 1972–

ARP, DENNIS J. ET AL.

AN INTRODUCTION TO THE INQUIRER II SYSTEM OF CONTENT ANALYSIS   COMPUTER STUDIES IN
THE HUMANITIES AND VERBAL BEHAVIOR 3: 40–45 JAN 1970

AUTOMATED TEXT EDITING – A BIBLIOGRAPHY WITH ABSTRACTS   NTIS/PS–76/O18L/8WAY 1976

BARKSDALE, G.L. JR. AND MEYER, W.B.

TPS, A TEXT PROCESSING SYSTEM – PRIMER AND REFERENCE MANUAL   AD–A021–763/8ST 1976

Fig. 4-7. Partial listing of FAMULUS bibliography.

The first control card, beginning with /ID/, is required by all FAMULUS programs. It identifies the particular file to be processed (i.e., printed, in the case of GALLEY). The /FIELDS/ control card identifies the individual fields to be printed for each entry in the bibliography. As shown in Fig. 4-7, AU is an author field, TI is a title field, PUB contains publication information, and DATE contains the date of publication. If only the author card and the title of each entry had been printed, the /FIELDS/ control card would appear as

/FIELDS/ (AU,TI)

The /PRINT BY SUBJECTS/ control card yields the particular print shown in Fig. 4-7. Alternatively, this card can be dropped if the different fields are to be printed on separate lines and the field labels (AU, TI, etc.) are to be shown. The /SELECT/ control card limits printing to the first five (1–5) entries in the file. Its omission would cause the entire file to be printed. Finally, the /NEW ID/ control card specifies the heading to be printed for the listing. Its omission would leave the file identification itself, given on the /ID card, to be printed as the heading.

4-2.2 Record Layout and File Creation

A FAMULUS *file* is a sequence of *records,* each record containing one or more *fields.* The record is identified as a single entry in a bibliography (for instance), and every record in such a file must contain the same configuration of fields. A file is usually created using 80-character punched cards (or card images on a terminal screen). The format of a punched card for such use is shown in Fig. 4-8.

Fig. 4-8. Format of a punched card for defining a field within FAMULUS record.

Columns 1-4 of a card are reserved for the field label (e.g., AU or TI in the example of Fig. 4-7). Columns 6-80 are used for the text of the field itself (e.g., the actual author or title of the entry). If the text exceeds columns 6-80, it may be continued in columns 6-80 of subsequent cards. Each such continuation card must be blank in columns 1-5. Figure 4-9 shows how the first five entries of the bibliography that was listed in Fig. 4-7 were originally encoded. When such a series of entries is punched, the following conventions must be strictly followed:

```
AU
TI    ALLC BULLETIN
PUB   ASOCIATION FOR LITERARY AND LINGUISTIC COMPUTING
DATE  1973-
KEYS

AU
TI    AMERICAN JOURNAL OF COMPUTATIONAL LINGUISTICS
PUB
DATE  1972-
KEYS

AU    ARP, DENNIS J. ET AL.
TI    AN INTRODUCTION TO THE INQUIRER II SYSTEM OF CONTENT ANALYSIS
PUB   COMPUTER STUDIES IN THE HUMANITIES AND VERBAL BEHAVIOR 3: 40-45
DATE  JAN 1970
KEYS

AU
TI    AUTOMATED TEXT EDITING - A BIBLIOGRAPHY WITH ABSTRACTS
PUB   NTIS/PS-76/0181/8WAY
DATE  1976
KEYS

AU    BARKSDALE, G.L. JR. AND MEYER, W.B.
TI    TPS, A TEXT PROCESSING SYSTEM - PRIMER AND REFERENCE MANUAL
PUB   AD-A021-763/8ST
DATE  1976
KEYS
```

Fig. 4-9. Encoding of bibliography entries.

    (1)   Each entry must be separated from the next by a blank card.

    (2)   Within an entry, its fields must be presented in the same order that they are defined for the file at the time the file is created.

To create the file, the punched cards must be placed immediately after the following control cards as input to the EDIT program:

```
/ID/file name
/FIELDS/(field names)
/ORIGINAL/
/CITATIONS/
```

Here, the "file name" may be any name that is appropriate to the nature of the file (and by which the file will be subsequently known). The "field names" are the names of the individual fields that will be in columns 1-4 of the individual entries, and in the same order that they will appear within an entry. The /ORIGINAL/ and /CITATIONS/ control cards are required to identify that the file is new, and that the individual entries ("citations") are provided on cards in the present run. Output of the EDIT program includes a listing of the records in the file, as shown in Fig. 4-10.

```
1   TI     ALLC BULLETIN
    PUB    ASOCIATION FOR LITERARY AND LINGUISTIC COMPUTING
    DATE   1973-

2   TI     AMERICAN JOURNAL OF COMPUTATIONAL LINGUISTICS
    DATE   1972-

3   AU     ARP, DENNIS J. ET AL.
    TI     AN INTRODUCTION TO THE INQUIRER II SYSTEM OF CONTENT ANALYSIS
    PUB    COMPUTER STUDIES IN THE HUMANITIES AND VERBAL BEHAVIOR 3: 40-45
    DATE   JAN 1970

4   TI     AUTOMATED TEXT EDITING - A BIBLIOGRAPHY WITH ABSTRACTS
    PUB    NTIS/PS-76/0181/8WAY
    DATE   1976

5   AU     BARKSDALE, G.L. JR. AND MEYER, W.B.
    TI     TPS, A TEXT PROCESSING SYSTEM - PRIMER AND REFERENCE MANUAL
    PUB    AD-A021-763/8ST
    DATE   1976
```

Fig. 4-10. Partial listing of FAMULUS file.

4-2.3   File Editing, Sort, and Merge

Once the FAMULUS file is created, entries may be added, changed, or deleted by subsequently using the EDIT program. The file may also be sorted into alphabetical sequence by some field (such as author or title). Also, two similar files that have been so sorted may be "merged" to create a single file out of them. These functions permit ongoing maintenance of a bibliography after its original creation, without having to repeatedly create it each time a change occurs.

To add entries to an existing FAMULUS file, the following sequence of control cards is required:

/ID/file name
/CITATIONS/
⎰ entries to ⎱
⎱ be added ⎰

Here, the "file name" identifies the file, and the "entries to be added" denotes a deck of cards defining the entries that are to be added to the file. These are encoded using the same conventions that applied when the file was created (e.g., Fig. 4-9).

To change the values of fields within entries, the /REPLACE/ control card is used. Before any changes can be made, the file must already have been created and an EDIT or GALLEY listing should be in hand. On that listing, each record appears together with its FAMULUS-assigned record number. For example, see Fig. 4-10.

To change a field within a particular record, the following information must be provided on the /REPLACE/ control card:

(1)   the record number,
(2)   the label of the field to be changed,
(3)   the part of the field to be changed,
(4)   the new material to be inserted in that part.

For example, if we wish to change the title field of record number 3, in the listing shown in Fig. 4-10, so that THE is replaced by A, then we would write a /REPLACE/ card as

/REPLACE/(3)(TI)*THE*A*

To delete THE, we would replace it by "nothing":

/REPLACE/(3)(TI)*THE**

To effect this change in all of the first four records, we would say

/REPLACE/ (1-4)(TI)*THE**

We note finally that the /REPLACE/ function's specifications are applied throughout the selected field. That is, all occurrences of THE in the title field are deleted by the above specification. Thus, to effect only one instance of a string (like THE), enough of its surrounding context must be provided to distinguish it from all other instances.

To delete an entire record (or records) from the file, the identifying number(s) of the record(s) must be provided in a /DELETE/ control card. For instance, the following specifications are three equivalent ways of deleting records 1-5 from the file shown in Fig. 4-10:

/DELETE/(1,2,3,4,5)
/DELETE/(1-5)
/DELETE/(1,2-4,5)

To sort the entries of a file into alphabetical order by one or more fields, the SORT program is used. The /ID/ control card is used to identify the file to be sorted, and the /FIELDS/ control card is used to name the fields that will control the sort. For instance, if we wanted to sort the file that was created in Section 4-2 so that its records are alphabetically arranged by author and date of publication, we would give the following control information to the SORT program:

/ID/TEXT PROCESSING BIBLIOGRAPHY
/FIELDS/(AU,DATE)

Figure 4-11 shows the result of this sort for the five entries listed in Fig. 4-9. Note here that three of the five entries have blank authors, so that they appear

SORTED T. P. BIBLIOGRAPHY

1 TI AMERICAN JOURNAL OF COMPUTATIONAL LINGUISTICS
  DATE 1972-

2 TI ALLC BULLETIN
  PUB ASOCIATION FOR LITERARY AND LINGUISTIC COMPUTING
  DATE 1973-

3 TI AUTOMATED TEXT EDITING - A BIBLIOGRAPHY WITH ABSTRACTS
  PUB NTIS/PS-76/0181/8WAY
  DATE 1976

4 AU ARP, DENNIS J. ET AL.
  TI AN INTRODUCTION TO THE INQUIRER II SYSTEM OF CONTENT ANALYSIS
  PUB COMPUTER STUDIES IN THE HUMANITIES AND VERBAL BEHAVIOR 3: 40-45
  DATE JAN 1970

5 AU BARKSDALE, G.L. JR. AND MEYER, W.B.
  TI TPS, A TEXT PROCESSING SYSTEM - PRIMER AND REFERENCE MANUAL
  PUB AD-A021-763/8ST
  DATE 1976

Fig. 4-11. Sorted file by author and date.

together and are arranged by date only. In a sort of this kind, blank fields will always precede nonblank fields in the final ordering.

To merge two files into a single file, the MERGE program is used. It requires that the two input files be sorted a priori and into the same sequence (e.g., by author and date). The only control cards that are needed for the merge are two /ID/ cards to identify the input files and a /NEW ID/ card to name the output (merged) file.

4-2.4 Information Retrieval Functions: SEARCH, COUNT, VOCAB, and Automatic Keywording

The power of information retrieval systems lies in their facilities for searching files and identifying records that satisfy user-specified search criteria. Additionally, descriptive information about the vocabulary used in a file, such as word frequencies, is also valuable. Finally, the automatic generation of all keywords that occur in some field of each record can relieve some of the tedium of maintaining and retrieving relevant entries in a bibliography. All of these facilities are available in FAMULUS.

To search a file and retrieve all records that satisfy certain specified criteria, the SEARCH program is used. To define these search criteria, the /SEARCH/ control card is used. To illustrate, suppose we want to retrieve all records in our TEXT PROCESSING BIBLIOGRAPHY file with an AUTHOR field that contains GNUGNOLI or a DATE field that contains 1974. This would be specified as

```
/ID/TEXT PROCESSING BIBLIOGRAPHY
/SEARCH/GNUGNOLI(AU) | 1974 (DATE)
```

in the /SEARCH/ control card, the symbol | denoting the logical connector "or." Thus, when connecting two parts of a /SEARCH/ control card, | specifies that either of the parts can be present (e.g., either an author field that contains GNUGNOLI or a date field that contains 1974) in a record for that record to be selected.

Similarly, the symbol & denotes the logical connector "and." For example, the /SEARCH/ control card

```
/SEARCH/GNUGNOLI(AU) & 1974(DATE)
```

will cause selection of all entries that contain GNUGNOLI in the author field and 1974 in the date field.

The symbol &, |, and ⌐ can be combined to form more complex /SEARCH/ specifications. For example,

```
/SEARCH/(GNUGNOLI(AU) | NGUYEN(AU)) & 1974(DATE)
```

selects all entries with GNUGNOLI or NGUYEN in their author field and 1974 in their DATE field. Parentheses are used here to designate that the | operator take precedence over &. If the parentheses had been omitted, as in

```
/SEARCH/GNUGNOLI(AU) | NGUYEN(AU) & 1974(DATE)
```

the & operator would take precedence over |. Thus, all entries that have either GNUGNOLI in their author field or both NGUYEN in their author field and 1974 in their DATE field would be retrieved.

Any series of symbols, whether it designates part of a field or an entire field, can be given in a /SEARCH/ specification. This can sometimes be useful. For instance, if we say

```
/SEARCH/197(DATE)
```

all entries that have 197 in the DATE field will be selected, thus effectively identifying the decade 1970–1979.

The COUNT and VOCAB programs both provide an alphabetized list of the words that occur within selected fields in all records of a file. Additionally, the COUNT program tabulates the number of occurrences of each word in the selected field.

Such "vocabulary lists" are useful aids to a number of text processing tasks, such as data validation, thesaurus building, and elementary research (statistical analysis) on the file's contents.

Figure 4-12 shows part of the result of executing the COUNT program on the title (TI) field of the example bibliography that was introduced in Fig. 4-9. The VOCAB program yields identically the same result, except that the word counts (numbers) do not appear.

```
            V O C A B U L A R Y   W O R D S

-              2  5.71    BULLETIN        1  2.86    OF           2  5.71
A              2  5.71    COMPUTATIONAL   1  2.86    PRIMER       1  2.86
ABSTRACTS      1  2.86    CONTENT         1  2.86    PROCESSING   1  2.86
ALLC           1  2.86    EDITING         1  2.86    REFERENCE    1  2.86
AMERICAN       1  2.86    II              1  2.86    SYSTEM       2  5.71
AN             1  2.86    INQUIRER        1  2.86    TEXT         2  5.71
ANALYSIS       1  2.86    INTRODUCTION    1  2.86    THE          1  2.86
AND            1  2.86    JOURNAL         1  2.86    TO           1  2.86
AUTOMATED      1  2.86    LINGUISTICS     1  2.86    TPS          1  2.86
BIBLIOGRAPHY   1  2.86    MANUAL          1  2.86    WITH         1  2.86

                                   STATISTICS OF WORD TYPES

VOCABULARY WORDS...
DISTRIBUTION OF WORD LENGTHS
        2  4  3  3  3  0  3  3  4  3  1
        1  2  1

NUMBER OF VOCABULARY WORD TYPES =   30
AVERAGE LENGTH = 6.2
MAXIMUM LENGTH = 13
MAXIMUM POSSIBLE = 40

DICTIONARY SIZE...
NUMBER OF ENTRIES =       30       MAXIMUM =  4500
NUMBER OF CHARACTERS =   187       MAXIMUM = 45000

                                   STATISTICS OF WORD TOKENS

VOCABULARY WORDS...
DISTRIBUTION OF WORD FREQUENCIES
     R     N     F(N)    SIGMA(F(N))    N*F(N)    SIGMA(N*F(N))
     1     2       5          5           10           10
     2     1      25         30           25           35

AVERAGE FREQUENCY = 15.00
MAXIMUM FREQUENCY = 25
NUMBER OF VOCABULARY WORD TOKENS =  35

FILE SIZE...
TOTAL NUMBER OF WORD TOKENS =       35
TOTAL NUMBER OF CHARACTERS =       201
```

Fig. 4-12. Sample output from the COUNT program.

Automatic keywording is provided through the KEY program. When invoked, the KEY program places all terms that have been designated as keywords and that occur in one or more selected fields automatically into another field, which has been designated as the *key field*. The keywords are listed on a /GO LIST/ card, the selected fields are given on a /FIELDS/ card, and the key field is identified on a /KEY FIELD/ card. Absence of a /GO LIST/ card will cause all words from the selected fields to be keyworded. A /STOP LIST/ card can, in addition, be used to identify words (such as A, AN, and THE) to be excluded from the keywording operation.

```
1   TI     ALLC BULLETIN
    PUB    ASOCIATION FOR LITERARY AND LINGUISTIC COMPUTING
    DATE   1973-

2   TI     AMERICAN JOURNAL OF COMPUTATIONAL LINGUISTICS
    DATE   1972-

3   AU     ARP, DENNIS J. ET AL.
    TI     AN INTRODUCTION TO THE INQUIRER II SYSTEM OF CONTENT ANALYSIS
    PUB    COMPUTER STUDIES IN THE HUMANITIES AND VERBAL BEHAVIOR 3: 40-45
    DATE   JAN 1970

4   TI     AUTOMATED TEXT EDITING - A BIBLIOGRAPHY WITH ABSTRACTS
    PUB    NTIS/PS-76/0181/8WAY
    DATE   1976
    KEYS   TEXT

5   AU     BARKSDALE, G.L. JR. AND MEYER, W.B.
    TI     TPS, A TEXT PROCESSING SYSTEM - PRIMER AND REFERENCE MANUAL
    PUB    AD-A021-763/8ST
    DATE   1976
    KEYS   TEXT
```

Fig. 4-13. Automatic keywording example.

In the example shown in Fig. 4-13, we have performed automatic keywording on the title (TI) field of the sample bibliography that was introduced in Fig. 4-9. Only the words TEXT, STRING, and WORD have been keyworded, and the new field KEYS has been added to store all occurrences of these keywords from the title. The control cards for this operation are

```
/ID/TEXT PROCESSING BIBLIOGRAPHY/
/FIELDS/(TI)
/KEY FIELD/(KEYS)(,)
/GO LIST/TEXT*STRING*WORD
```

Note in this example that the comma is used to separate adjacent keywords in the KEYS field.

4-2.5 Generating Indexes and Concordances

FAMULUS can be used to generate an alphabetical index of terms in the description field of a file. It also has facilities to generate a KWIC index, or concordance, of words in a file.

For an index, the INDEX program is used, together with the following control card:

```
/DESCRIPTION FIELD/(field name)
```

This card serves to identify the field, by way of the "field name," which will supply the words that are to occur in the index. For example, an index for all titles from the bibliography file in Fig. 4-9 can be generated by the control cards

```
/ID/TEXT PROCESSING BIBLIOGRAPHY
/DESCRIPTION FIELD/ (TI)
```

For a concordance, the KWIC program is used, together with the /FIELDS/ control card to define the field(s) that will supply the text from which the concordance will be generated.

Optionally, the /STOP LIST/ and /GO LIST/ control cards may be used to specify excluded and included words, respectively. (This is the same capability that was illustrated in Fig. 4-4 for another concordance-generation program.) For example, if we want a concordance of all words that occur in titles of our sample bibliography (see Fig. 4-9), excluding all articles (A, AN, and THE), we would use the following control cards with the KWIC program:

```
/ID/TEXT PROCESSING BIBLIOGRAPHY
/FIELDS/ (TI)
/STOP LIST/A*AN*THE
```

Figure 4-14 shows part of the concordance that occurs from this specification, applied to the sample entries shown in Fig. 4-9.

4-2.6 Deck Setup for Running FAMULUS

To run FAMULUS on an IBM 360 or 370 computer, the general deck setup shown in Fig. 4-15 is required. The exact form of the job card will vary among installations, but the rest of the deck is reasonably universal in format. For more information on the input and output files for a FAMULUS run, the reader should consult his or her computer center staff. It should be noted here that the input file for a FAMULUS run may be on cards, tape, or disk. The same is true for the output file. The deck setup shown in Fig. 4-15 is for creating a FAMULUS file on disk from the series of bibliography entries that appear in Fig. 4-9. Here the EDIT program was used, and its printed output is shown in Fig. 4-10.

```
4                         AUTOMATED TEXT EDITING — A BIBLIOGRAPHY WITH ABSTRACTS
5            TPS, A TEXT PROCESSING SYSTEM — PRIMER AND REFERENCE MANUAL

4       AUTOMATED TEXT EDITING — A BIBLIOGRAPHY WITH ABSTRACTS
                                                 ABSTRACTS
1                                       ALLC BULLETIN
                                        ALLC
2                             AMERICAN JOURNAL OF COMPUTATIONAL LINGUISTICS
                                        AMERICAN
3   AN INTRODUCTION TO THE INQUIRER II SYSTEM OF CONTENT ANALYSIS
                                                 ANALYSIS
5            TPS, A TEXT PROCESSING SYSTEM — PRIMER AND REFERENCE MANUAL
                                                 AND

4                         AUTOMATED TEXT EDITING — A BIBLIOGRAPHY WITH ABSTRACTS
                                                 AUTOMATED

4                         AUTOMATED TEXT EDITING — A BIBLIOGRAPHY WITH ABSTRACTS
                                                 BIBLIOGRAPHY
```

Fig. 4-14. Concordance sample generated by KWIC program.

```
//TERMFAM1 JOB (0060,7022),TUCKER,CLASS=A,TIME=2
/*USERID ACCADM1
// EXEC PGM=IEFBR14
//DD DD DSN=ACC.AT.FAMSAM,VOL=REF=ACC.DATASET,UNIT=SYSDA,
//   DISP=(OLD,DELETE)
// EXEC FAMULUS,PROG=EDIT,OUTDATA='ACC.AT.FAMSAM',OUTREF='ACC.DATASET',
// SPACE=2
//GO.SYSIN DD *
/ID/TEXT PROCESSING BIBLIOGRAPHY
/FIELDS/(AU,TI,PUB,DATE,KEYS)
/ORIGINAL/
/CITATIONS/
AU
TI    ALLC BULLETIN
PUB   ASOCIATION FOR LITERARY AND LINGUISTIC COMPUTING
DATE  1973-
KEYS

AU
TI    AMERICAN JOURNAL OF COMPUTATIONAL LINGUISTICS
PUB
DATE  1972-
KEYS

AU    ARP, DENNIS J. ET AL.
TI    AN INTRODUCTION TO THE INQUIRER II SYSTEM OF CONTENT ANALYSIS
PUB   COMPUTER STUDIES IN THE HUMANITIES AND VERBAL BEHAVIOR 3: 40-45
DATE  JAN 1970
KEYS

AU
TI    AUTOMATED TEXT EDITING - A BIBLIOGRAPHY WITH ABSTRACTS
PUB   NTIS/PS-76/0181/8WAY
DATE  1976
KEYS

AU    BARKSDALE, G.L. JR. AND MEYER, W.B.
TI    TPS, A TEXT PROCESSING SYSTEM - PRIMER AND REFERENCE MANUAL
PUB   AD-A021-763/8ST
DATE  1976
KEYS

//
```

Fig. 4-15. Example of a complete FAMULUS run.

It is unfortunate that the FAMULUS package is not available on non-IBM machines. Our illustrations are closely tied to the IBM vernacular, which limits their generality and usefulness to readers who do not have easy access to an IBM computer. This is true of most current text processing packages; none is so widely used that it has been implemented and supported on more than one computer species.

4-3 CMS Editor for Interactive Text Editing

In Section 4-2, we saw an example of text file maintenance that takes place essentially in *batch* mode. That is, additions and corrections to a text are collected in a batch, and then are applied to the file in a single run.

In many text processing applications the text requires such frequent and/or detailed maintenance that batching is not particularly convenient or effective. That is, the occurrence of errors is so frequent and the cost of keying the corrections is so high that the results obtained are difficult to cost-justify.

The last few years has seen rapid growth of *interactive* text editing packages. That is, text additions and changes are keyed at an interactive terminal that is connected to the computer, and are thus immediately entered into the text file. This process is more convenient than traditional methods that use punched cards and batch processing.

In this section, we illustrate the flavor of interactive text editing by using some of the facilities of IBM's CMS Editor, which runs under the VM/370 operating system. Our choice of the IBM Editor as our basis for illustration is dictated strictly by convenience. Similar editors are available on DEC, Burroughs, Honeywell, CDC, Univac, and other computers as well. Nevertheless, we hope that the reader will, in this section, gain an appreciation of the overall value of interactive text editing.

This section is divided into four parts. Section 4-3.1 discusses the creation and listing of a text file under CMS. Section 4-3.2 discusses various text storage and retrieval functions that CMS supports. In Section 4-3.3, we illustrate some of the more useful text search and editing functions. The interface between CMS and batch processing functions of the IBM computer is illustrated in Section 4-3.4. As a vehicle for illustration, we use the example text that appears in Fig. 1-2 of Chapter 1.

4-3.1 Sample CMS Text Creation and Listing

A typical CMS terminal is pictured in Fig. 1-6. The keyboard of a terminal is similar to that of an ordinary typewriter. Unlike a keypunch machine, many terminals permit the use of lower-case letters, in addition to uppercase. However, the lowercase alphabet on a terminal may or may not be activated. That is, the entry of "h" and "H" (for example) may deliver the same code to the computer. In this section, we assume that to be the case.

The "prompt" character in CMS is the period, which appears at the beginning of a line on the screen. The user cannot enter a message until after this character has appeared. Figure 4-16 shows part of a typical CMS dialogue between the computer and a user. The reader should be able to distinguish that which the user has entered from that which the computer has provided, by observing the presence or absence of the period at the beginning of each line.

Each separate text that is created and/or manipulated under CMS must first be identified as a CMS file. Each time a text is accessed, it is referenced by way of its "file name" and "file type." A file name can be any sequence that begins with a letter (A-Z) and contains eight or fewer letters and/or digits (0-9). The

```
.delete 3
.t
 /*
.up
 /*
.i
 INPUT:
.//go.data dd *
 EDIT:
.t
 //GO.DATA DD *
.top
 TOP:
.t*
 TOP:
 //TERMCONC JOB (0060,7022),TUCKER,CLASS=A,TIME=2
 /*USERID ACCADM1
 // EXEC GUKWIC
 //GO.$ORTPARM DD *
  CORE=80000
```

Fig. 4-16. Part of a typical CMS dialogue.

file type is similarly defined and in addition certain file types have special meanings in CMS. Some of these are described below:

CMS file type	Special meaning
EXEC	A file that is a "CMS program" and serves to extend the functions built into CMS.
FORTRAN	A file that is a FORTRAN program.
PLIOPT	A file that is a PL/I program.
COBOL	A file that is a COBOL program.

When a file with one of these special file types is defined in CMS, it inherits certain additional characteristics. For instance, the PLIOPT file type endows a file with the ability to be immediately compiled and executed from the terminal. For our purposes, these special file types have no immediate usefulness. Thus they should be viewed by the reader as simply "off limits" for use in defining a file type.

To create a CMS file that contains the text shown in Fig. 1-2, we must first assign it a file name and file type, say SAMPLE TEXT. Next, we may encode the text at the terminal, one line at a time, following the sequence shown below:

```
.edit sample text
NEW FILE:
EDIT:
.input
INPUT:

.
```

In this sequence, we have entered "edit mode" and have identified the file name and file type of the file that we wish to edit. In response, CMS tells us that it is a NEW FILE (i.e., there is no other file in the system with the same name and type). When in edit mode, we may create and/or modify any file. To add a series of lines to a file, we must enter "input mode." That is the second action we specified in the above sequence. In response, CMS enters input mode (IN-PUT:) and the prompt on the next line indicates that the system is ready to receive the first additional line of text. The lines are then entered as shown in Fig. 4-17. Once the file is created, the operator can return from input mode to edit mode by keying an empty line (i.e., by hitting RETURN twice in succession).

To save a copy of the file just created and return from edit mode, the user types FILE. Once the file has been saved, the operator may retrieve it for further manipulation at a later time.

To obtain a printed listing of this file, the user types PRINT SAMPLE TEXT. To create a punched card deck of the file, the user types PUNCH SAMPLE TEXT. In either of these cases, the listing or deck must be retrieved from the batch distribution area at the computer center. This area may not be physically close to the terminal from which the listing or deck was requested.

4-3.2 Text Storage and Retrieval

Once a file is created, its most recent version is always accessible from the terminal. The CMS instruction

EDIT file name file type

retrieves that version for examination or modification, while the instruction

SAVE

saves the most recent version for future use. The SAVE instruction can only be issued from edit mode. In this case, the file name and file type are implicitly understood to be the same as they were at the time edit mode was entered (via EDIT file name file type).

To save both the previous version and the current version of a file during an edit session, the SAVE instruction can be provided with a different file name and file type. For example, suppose that we wish to add another paragraph to the text that we had created in the previous section and stored as SAMPLE TEXT. Then we would proceed in the following steps:

(1) Type EDIT SAMPLE TEXT to retrieve the original text.
(2) Type BOT to position ourselves at the bottom of the original text.

```
R:
.edit sample text
NEW FILE:
EDIT:
.input
INPUT:
. The geographical distribution of research and development        sam00010
.activities is a source of increasing interest and concern .  We are  sam00020
.just beginning to understand the full impact of large scale          sam00030
.nationwide R&D programs of the last decade .  The R&D programs have  sam00040
.had a profound effect on economic growth and prosperity in the       sam00050
.community , state , and region .  At every level these activities    sam00060
.benefit .
.EDIT:
.save
EDIT:
.quit
R:
```

Fig. 4-17. Creating a CMS file in input mode.

(3)   Type UP to position ourselves (upward) to the line before the bottom.

(4)   Type INPUT to enter input mode (and enable addition of new lines at the bottom of the file).

(5)   Type the additional lines, one at a time, followed by an empty line (to return from input mode to edit mode).

(6)   Return from edit mode after saving the new version by typing SAVE SAMPLE TEXT2 and QUIT.

After these steps are completed, we have two different files, SAMPLE TEXT and SAMPLE TEXT2. Note that INPUT is used to add lines to a text beginning at a certain position, as well as to create an entirely new text. Addition of lines, as well as most other editing functions to be discussed below, always take place at a particular vertical position, or line, within the file. A priori, the position TOP is the top of the file and BOT is the bottom of the file. The top precedes the first line, and the bottom follows the last line. To position oneself at either of these positions, one types TOP or BOT accordingly. Thus the INPUT instruction designates that lines are to be added immediately after the currently accessed line.

This sample also illustrates that the SAVE and QUIT instructions are equivalent to the FILE instruction that was introduced in Section 4-2. The SAVE instruction may be used by itself when we want to save the current version of a file and then remain in edit mode to perform more modifications of the file.

Once in edit mode, we can position ourselves at any line of the file. The following instructions are available for such positioning:

Instruction	Meaning (resulting position)
TOP	Top of file.
BOTTOM	Bottom of file.
NEXT	Next line downward (from the current position).
UP	Next line upward.
NEXT n	Move downward n lines from the current position.
UP n	Move upward n lines.

The previous example used the UP instruction to move upward by one line from the bottom of the file. This is equivalent, then, to UP 1. Similarly, five occurrences of the instruction NEXT will arrive at the same position as the instruction NEXT 5, and so forth. To find out what line is the current line during an edit session, simply type TYPE. To type a series of (say) five lines, beginning with the current one, type TYPE 5.

Most of these instructions can be abbreviated. The CMS user quickly memorizes these abbreviations because of the heavy usage they receive. The allowable abbreviations for the instructions given above are as follows:

Instruction	Abbreviation
EDIT	E
TOP	TOP
BOTTOM	BOT
NEXT	N
UP	U
TYPE	T

As new instructions are introduced below, we shall denote their abbreviations by underlining the required letters. For instance, the fact that EDIT may be abbreviated as E will be denoted by E̲DIT.

In contrast with adding lines to a text, we sometimes wish to delete one or more lines. To delete (say) five lines from the text, beginning with the current one, the instruction

D̲E̲L̲E̲TE 5

can be used. Alternatively, if we want to replace the current line with an entirely new line, we would type R̲E̲P̲L̲ACE followed by the new line. In effect, a R̲E̲P̲L̲ACE instruction is equivalent to a D̲E̲L̲E̲TE 1 followed by an INPUT of one line. However, the D̲E̲L̲E̲TE instruction leaves the current position as the line following the line deleted. Thus, to properly position oneself for INPUT in the same position as a previous deletion, the deletion must be followed by an UP instruction. The following example illustrates this point:

Text before	Instruction sequence	Text after
→ LINE 1 LINE 2 LINE 3	(a) DELETE 2 INPUT LINE 1A	LINE 3 → LINE 1A
	(b) DELETE 2 UP INPUT LINE 1A	→ LINE 1A LINE 3

Here, the arrow (→) indicates the current line. Sequence (a) results in LINE 1A's insertion after LINE 3, while sequence (b) inserts LINE 1A before LINE 3.

4-3.3   Automatic Text Search and Modification

When in edit mode, it is often awkward to locate a line of text by moving up and /or down a fixed number of lines. Often we would like to search for the first line that contains a given string, such as the word 'HEALTH', the phrase 'In Conclusion', or the punctuation '('.

CMS provides this type of search with the search command. The search command is specified by a slash (/) followed immediately by the string to be located. For example, if we wanted to search for the next line (beyond the current one) that contains the string 'HEALTH', we would type

/HEALTH

If HEALTH appears in the ensuing text, then the line on which it appears will be displayed and become the current line. If not, the response EOF will occur, indicating that HEALTH does not appear in the remainder of the text and the "end of file" has been reached. In this event, the current line becomes the bottom of the file.

We must be careful, in specifying a search, to distinguish exactly what we are looking for. For instance, the specification /HEALTH will leave us at the first occurrence of the string HEALTH, which may or may not be a separate word. Any of the following phrases successfully terminate the search:

PUBLIC HEALTH DOCTRINE
HEALTH—RELATED OCCUPATIONS
HEALTHY CHILDREN

Another constraint that the system imposes is that the search looks at each line of text as a separate entity. Therefore, if an occurrence of the word HEALTH is split between two lines in the file, as in

. . . PUBLIC HEAL
TH DOCTRINE . . .

this occurrence will not be found by a search. For this reason, it may be advisable to initially enter the text in such a way that no word is split between two lines.

To modify a text, the *change* and *replace* functions are available. The change function allows one to change any particular string in the current line to another string, while the replace function allows one to replace the entire current line by a new line.

The change function is specified as:

CHANGE/ old string/new string/

Here, "old string" designates the string to be replaced and "new string" designates the string that will replace it. For example, suppose that the current line is

PUBLIC HELTH DOCTRINE

and we want to correct the spelling of the second word. To do this, we can say

C/E/EA/

which designates that the first occurrence of E in the line will be replaced by EA, giving the following result:

PUBLIC HEALTH DOCTRINE

The change function always operates from left to right in a line, so that the leftmost occurrence of a designated string is always affected. Care must be taken, therefore, to unambiguously designate the desired string. For example, if we wish to change the above line to

PUBLIC HEALTH DOCTRINES

the specification C/E/ES/ is not good enough.This will leave the following instead:

PUBLIC HESALTH DOCTRINE

To isolate the final E, we must give a string that uniquely identifies it, as

C/NE/NES/

Often the change function is useful to insert or delete blank spaces in a line. For instance, the special designation

C//ƀ/

says "replace the leftmost occurrence of the null (empty) string by a blank space." That occurrence always precedes the left end of the line, by definition, and so the net effect is to insert a blank space at the beginning of the line.

The replace function is specified in the following way:

<u>REPLACE</u>ƀnewline

Here, "newline" designates the line that will replace the current line. For example, to correct the spelling error in the line

PUBLIC HELTH DOCTRINE

We can replace the line as follows:

REP PUBLIC HEALTH DOCTRINE

4-3.4 *Interface with Batch Processing*

In addition to its text editing facilities, CMS provides a link to the batch processing system. This allows the terminal user to directly "submit" a job to the batch system from the terminal. For this, a CMS file is prepared that looks exactly like a batch job, complete with JOB card, other control cards, and the text (data) to be used as input. Once this file is prepared the user sends, or "spools," it to the batch system by way of the following command:

SPOOL file name file type

This spares the user from the tedium of handling punched cards, while still providing access to all the software that is available in the batch system for text processing, such as FAMULUS, KWIC, and SCRIPT.

   To illustrate this interface, suppose we want to generate a concordance from the SAMPLE TEXT shown in Fig. 4-17. Then we would define another CMS file, say SAMPLE CONC, which contains not only the sample text, but also the entire collection of control card images that must accompany the text in order to obtain a concordance (see Fig. 4-3). The creation of this file is shown in Fig. 4-18.

   Most of these instructions should be familiar to the reader. The only additional instruction here is the GETFILE instruction. This instruction obtains a copy of

```
.edit sample conc
 EDIT:
./data
//GO.DATA DD *
.getfile sample text
 EOF REACHED
 BENEFIT .
.top
 TOP:
.t*
 TOP:
//TERMCONC JOB (0060,7022),TUCKER,CLASS=A,TIME=2
/*USERID ACCADM1
// EXEC GUKWIC
//GO.$ORTPARM DD *
 CORE=80000
 /*
//GO.DATA DD *
      THE GEOGRAPHICAL DISTRIBUTION OF RESEARCH AND DEVELOPMENT        SAM00010
 ACTIVITIES IS A SOURCE OF INCREASING INTEREST AND CONCERN .  WE ARE   SAM00020
 JUST BEGINNING TO UNDERSTAND THE FULL IMPACT OF LARGE SCALE           SAM00030
 NATIONWIDE R&D PROGRAMS OF THE LAST DECADE .   THE R&D PROGRAMS HAVE  SAM00040
 HAD A PROFOUND EFFECT ON ECONOMIC GROWTH AND PROSPERITY IN THE        SAM00050
 COMMUNITY , STATE , AND REGION .   AT EVERY LEVEL THESE ACTIVITIES    SAM00060
 BENEFIT .
 /*
//GO.SYSIN DD *
 CONCORDANCE FOR SAMPLE TEXT
 RECLNG=80
 TXTLNG=71
 IDPOS=72
 IDLNG=9

 //
 EOF:
.quit
 R;
```

Fig. 4-18. Creation of a CMS file for a batch job.

the entire file SAMPLE TEXT, and inserts it after the current line of the present file. After this job has been created, the instruction

```
SP SAMPLE CONC
```

will initiate a batch job that generates a concordance from the sample text. The concordance will be printed in hardcopy form and distributed exactly as if it had been submitted as a card deck. Thus, CMS provides an extremely convenient method of text editing and job submission.

4-4 SCRIPT for Text Formatting

SCRIPT was developed in the 1960s as a text processing package to aid in the preparation of manuscripts for publication: theses, papers, books, and other documents. It contains facilities that aid the author by automatically formatting each page of text and performing various mechanistic tasks such as the automatic generation of an index. Current versions of SCRIPT run on IBM 360 and 370 computers, under TSO and VM/CMS operating systems. Text formatting packages with similar capabilities have been developed for other computers, but the author is aware of no single package that is transferable among different computers.

4-4.1 Sample SCRIPT File and Printed Result

Any text to be formatted by SCRIPT must be presented as a sequential file. Embedded within the text are so-called control lines, which communicate formatting information to SCRIPT. A control line begins with the special character ''.'' followed by a two-letter symbol that identifies the nature of the command. For example, the command .US denotes that a word should be underscored, .SP denotes that a vertical space be inserted before the next line, and so forth.

To illustrate these conventions more fully, a sample SCRIPT input file and the resulting printed output are shown in Fig. 4-19 and 4-20, respectively. Here, much of the power of SCRIPT is illustrated, and the meaning of many control words is apparent from their effect on the output. Most notable among SCRIPT's functions is its ability to align text at the right margin, regardless of the spacing that occurs within its input representation.

4-4.2 Creation of SCRIPT Input Text

When preparing an input text for SCRIPT, the user provides two kinds of information: control words and the text itself. The input is typed either on a series of lines at the terminal or into a series of punched cards. In either case, each input line (card) may be terminated in either of two ways:

```
.tt 1 /SCRIPT/ SAMPLE TEXT / PAGE % /
.pp      The geographical distribution of research and development activities
is a source of increasing interest and concern.  We are just beginning
to understand the full impact of large scale nationwide R&D (*)
.fn begin
(*) research and development
.fn end
programs of the last decade.   The R&D programs have had a
.us profound
effect on economic growth and prosperity in the community, state, and region.
At every geographic level these activities benefit.
.cm the 3 items listed below should be indented.
.sp 1
.in 5
.of 4
.ce Employment, Prosperity, Education
.sp 1
1.  Employment, through more jobs and especially through more technical
jobs in the areas of science and engineering, with supporting
personnel.
.sp 1
.in 5
.of 4
2.  Business prosperity, through purchase of machinery and equipment
, plant facilities and office furniture, office space, etc., and
.sp 1
.in 5
.of 4
3.  Education, through modernization curricula and a closer alignment
between of training and the skills demanded in today's jobs.
.in 0
.pp      Each community, state, and region has different needs and different
resources -- manpower, equipment, leadership -- to meet these
needs.  Effective application of science and thechnology to satisfy
national needs must often focus an a variety of applications to the components
of national needs, i.e., specific local needs.
```

Fig. 4-19. Sample SCRIPT input text.

```
        The   geographical   distribution   of   research   and
development activities  is  a   source  of   increasing interest
and concern.    We are  just    beginning to understand the full
impact of large  scale nationwide R&D (*)    programs of the
last decade.   The R&D programs have had a profound effect on
economic growth and prosperity in the community,  state,   and
region.   At every geographic level these activities benefit.
```

```
            Employment, Prosperity, Education
```

```
            1.     Employment,    through   more   jobs   and
especially through more technical jobs in the areas
of   science    and   engineering,    with  supporting
personnel.
```

```
            2.    Business prosperity,  through  purchase  of
machinery  and equipment   ,   plant facilities  and
office furniture, office space, etc., and
```

```
            3.   Education, through modernization curricula and
a  closer alignment  between  of  training and   the
skills demanded in today's jobs.
```

```
        Each community,    state,   and   region has  different
needs  and  different resources  --   manpower,    equipment,
leadership -- to meet these needs.   Effective application of
science and thechnology to satisfy national needs must often
focus  an  a  variety of  applications  to  the components  of
national needs, i.e., specific local needs.
```

```
            --------------------
```

```
(*) research and development
```

Fig. 4-20. Printed output from sample SCRIPT input.

(1)   by reaching the physical end of the line (card),
(2)   by typing a semicolon (;) on the line (card).

A control word is needed whenever special formatting activity is to be performed by SCRIPT. Whenever it appears within the input, a control word must be at the beginning of an input line (card), or immediately after a semicolon on the line (card). A control word is distinguished by its unique form within a text. That is, it begins with a period and two letters.

Control words are obeyed by SCRIPT according to the position in which they appear within the input text. That is, the input text is taken by SCRIPT one line at a time, beginning with the first. As each line is encountered, the presence of a control word will produce a particular output formatting action, and then the ensuing text will be printed.

As an example, the following input shows the interaction of the .SP1 control word within the text itself:

```
FIRST PART; .SP1; SECOND PART
THIRD PART
```

Output from this input would appear as

```
FIRST PART
SECOND PART  THIRD PART
```

A more detailed example is shown in Fig. 4-19 and 4-20. In the following sections, we discuss the meanings of all individual control words that appear there. The reader should examine Fig. 4-19 first as an illustration of input text syntax. Note that the number of extra spaces that occur between words within a contiguous section of input text is immaterial, since SCRIPT will bring it all together in the output and automatically align left and right margins. This facilitates the insertion and deletion of words, sentences, and larger sections within the input text as the manuscript passes through different stages of refinement.

4-4.3 Layout of SCRIPT Page, Character Sets, and Related Control Words

The diagram in Fig. 4-21 shows how a SCRIPT output page is formatted, together with some control words that affect it. These control words are all present a priori by SCRIPT to *default* values, but may be reset from any location within the text. These control words, their meanings, and their default values are described below:

Control word	Default	Meaning
.PL	66	Page length, in lines per page
.LL	60	Line length, in characters per line.
.TM	6	Top margin; number of lines from top of page to first line of text.
.BM	6	Bottom margin; number of lines from last line of text to bottom of page.
.HS	1	Heading space; number of lines for heading on each page.
.FS	1	Footing space; number of lines for footing on each page.
.HM	1	Heading margin; number of lines between heading and top of text.
.FM	1	Footing margin; number of lines between bottom of text and footing.
.IN	0	Indent; number of spaces to indent the left margin.
.OF	0	Offset; number of spaces to offset the text to the right of the current left margin.

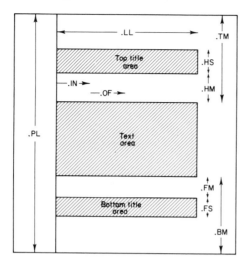

Fig. 4-21. SCRIPT output page layout.

The .PL and .LL control words can be used to quickly reformat a text to a different page size. The headings and footings are optional. Either one or both may be omitted by specifying one of the following, respectively:

.HS 0   or   .FS 0

In conjunction with the top margin is the top title, which can be specified by the .TT control word. Its format, for a one-line title, is

.TT/t1/t2/t3/

Here, t1, t2, and t3, respectively, denote titles to be adjusted at the left margin, centered, and adjusted at the right margin of the heading space. Any one of t1, t2, or t3 may be omitted. The presence of the special symbol % within any one of these will cause the current page number to be printed in its place. An illustration of the .TT control word appears in Fig. 4-19.

The .IN indent control word causes the left and right margins of the page to be temporarily indented a specified number (n) of spaces. Its form is

.IN n

This is useful when a body of text, such as a list, is to be aligned at a tab position rather than the left margin. The control word .IN 0 or just .IN, will turn off the effects of .IN n, and subsequent text will be realigned at the left margin.

The .OF (offset) control word causes all but the first line of a section to be indented a specified number (n) of spaces, beginning at the current position indicated by the most recent .IN control word. It has the form

.OF n

If n is omitted, the effect is the same as .OF 0. Furthermore, the first subsequent occurrence of the .IN control word will cancel the current offset specification.

Thus, .IN and .OF can work together, and .IN has a higher "priority" than .OF. An illustration of their use appears in Fig. 4-19.

4-4.4   Additional SCRIPT Control Words and Their Effects

SCRIPT supports a variety of formatting capabilities. Here, we introduce a few of the more common options so that the reader may gain an appreciation for their power. The following control words are presented and illsutrated in the paragraphs below:

Control word	Purpose
.CE	Centering of headings
.CM	Including a comment in the text
.FN	Defining footnotes
.SP	Skipping lines
.US	Underscoring text

A text may be centered by using the .CE control word. It can be given in one of the following forms:

.CE text
.CE n

Here, "text" denotes the text to be centered on a single line, while "n" denotes the number of following lines that should be centered. Examples are shown in Fig. 4-19.

From time to time, the SCRIPT user needs to write a descriptive comment or two within the text which will help document, for instance, a particularly complicated sequence of control words. The comment is provided as follows:

.CM comment

The comment will not appear in the output text, as shown in the example of Figs. 4-19 and 4-20.

The automatic footnote facility of SCRIPT is useful when preparing a paper that contains references to published works. Basically, the footnote is embedded between control words:

```
.FN BEGIN
footnote
.FN END
```

It is placed immediately after the reference to it in the input text. SCRIPT will lift the footnote and automatically place it within the bottom title area when the end of the page is reached. This facility is illustrated in Figs. 4-19 and 4-20.

Whenever one or more blank lines is needed between adjacent sections of output text, the .SP control word is used:

```
.SP n
```

Here, "n" denotes the desired number of blank lines. For instance, .SP 1 appears in the input text for Fig. 4-19, and its effect is shown in Fig. 4-20.

Occasionally, one or more words of text should be underscored when they are printed. To achieve this, the word is preceded by the .US control word. For example, the statement .US TEXT PROCESSING will result in the output

TEXT PROCESSING

Another example of underscoring is given in Figs. 4-19 and 4-20.

Questions and Exercises

1. Identify the principal advantage of a text processing package over a programming language for text processing. Are there situations in which a programming language would be preferable to a package? Explain.

2. Develop a single concordance-generation program in either PL/1 or SNOBOL.

3. Develop a program, in PL/1 or SNOBOL, that prints an alphabetized list of all words that occur in a text, together with their frequencies of occurrence. Compare this program with the concordance program, in terms of its specific programming tasks.

4. For the FAMULUS file shown in Fig. 4-7, show what control cards are needed to perform each of the following functions:

   (a)   Print the file, but only the TI (title) and DATE fields of each record.

   (b)   Replace in the file all DATE fields of the form 19xx to the form 'xx. For example, if a date is 1978, it should change to '78.

   (c)   Sort and print the file in order by DATE and TI (title), so that records are chronologically listed, and alphabetized within each year.

   (d)   Search the file and print all records that contain the word TEXT or STRING in their title, and were published since 1970.

5. What facility in FAMULUS is similar in its purpose to the program in Exercise 3?

6. What is automatic keywording?

7. What feature in FAMULUS is similar to the "excluded word list" in the KWIC package?

8. If you have access to an interactive text editor that is different from CMS, learn about it and compare its facilities with those of CMS.

9. Use the CMS Editor (or the editor to which you have access) to accomplish the following tasks:

(a) Create a file that contains the text in Fig. 1-2.

(b) Search the text for all sentence endings (occurrences of period, question mark, or exclamation mark), and concatenate each with the word that precedes it. For instance, change

THIS IS THE END

to

THIS IS THE END.

(c) Save this modified file, and print a hardcopy version of it.

10. Modify the SCRIPT input text in Fig. 4-19 so that it will be printed on a page size of 5x7 inches (rather than 8½x11 inches). Assume that 10 characters per inch will be printed horizontally and 6 lines per inch will be printed vertically.

11. Create a SCRIPT input text that is a poem of your choice. prepare it so that each line of a verse will begin on a separate print line, adjacent verses will be separated by a blank line, and any line of verse that exceeds one print line will have its second line indented. Creation of this text is most conveniently done using CMS.

12. Write a PL/1 or SNOBOL program that will, given an input text, print it so that each line is adjusted to left and right margins, and no word is split between two lines. Assume a line length of 60 characters and page length of 54 lines. Compare this exercise with the use of SCRIPT for the same purpose.

Chapter 5

Literature Review

The foregoing chapters have presented a reasonably varied selection of text processing languages, packages, and applications. In this chapter, we give a broader view of recent work in these areas. Because the amount of published material in text processing is immense, we present only a representative sample of recent articles for reference. We expect that this sample will provide the interested reader with enough material to pursue further research in any of these areas in greater depth.

For purposes of organization, this review is divided into five sections: Section 5-1 reviews the use of languages other than PL/I and SNOBOL for text processing. Section 5-2 briefly reviews text editors, formatters, and bibliographic information retrieval packages. Section 5-3 gives references on the use and results of computer-based concordance generation. Other language research topics, notably content analysis and machine translation, are briefly reviewed in Section 5-4. Section 5-5 provides references to additional sources of information that the interested reader can consult in order to remain current with the use of computers in text processing.

It is important to emphasize that this review does not cover several topics that are tangentially associated with text processing. Among these topics are computer graphics, artificial intelligence, data base management, operating systems, compilers, simulation, and computer-aided instruction. We also exclude, for purposes of brevity, such topics as computer-generated music, art, and poetry, computer animation, and statistical applications of the computer in the social, behavioral, and management sciences. These topics would properly be included in a broader review of the uses of computers in the humanities.

5-1.   Programming Languages for Text Processing

In Chapter 2 we explored the use of PL/I for writing text processing programs, and in Chapter 3 we did the same for SNOBOL. Although these two may be the best-suited langauges for text processing, the following languages have also been successfully used:

```
ALGOL       FORTRAN
APL         LISP
C           PASCAL
COBOL
```

Although ALGOL was originally designed for mathematical programming applications, recent versions of the language include text processing facilities as well. Hann (28) discusses the use of ALGOL for linguistic programming. Many texts and references are available that teach ALGOL. In addition, the programming language PASCAL is very similar to ALGOL in its features, and would thus be equally useful for text processing. The programming style (syntax) of ALGOL and PASCAL is similar to that of PL/I.

APL is also used principally for mathematical applications, particularly those that make heavy use of arrays. Nevertheless, APL has been used in text processing. For example, Bingham (7) discusses its use in the development of an on-line text editor. The programming style of APL is quite compact, in comparison with that of PL/I and SNOBOL. That is, a typical 100-statement PL/I program can be written in APL using fewer than ten statements. This expressive power results mainly from APL's extensive built-in array manipulation functions. For the uninitiated, APL programs tend to be more difficult to read (because of their compactness) than equivalent PL/I programs.

C is a programming language that was designed principally for systems programming applications. Although C has some syntactic similarity with PL/I, its built-in functions are more closely associated with those of a machine (or assembly) language. Nevertheless, Kelly (37) reports that C has been used in the programming of an interactive text editor for the UNIX Time Sharing Operating System.

COBOL was developed principally for programming in business data processing applications. Recent versions of COBOL have, however, been augmented to include a modest set of text processing facilities, notably the STRING and UNSTRING statements. Also, COBOL is widely known among professional programmers and supported by all major computer manufacturers. Compared with other languages, however, COBOL ranks low in its usefulness for text processing.

FORTRAN is strictly a language for mathematical applications. In order to do any appreciable text processing with FORTRAN, one must extend the language by adding character string processing functions. The most widely known FORTRAN extension that includes such functions is WATFIV. Carbrey (12) reports an extension to the CDC 6000 FORTRAN language that contains subroutines and functions for character manipulation. The use of FORTRAN in text processing is shown by Messina and Hilsenrath (44), who describe a set of edit-insertion programs for automatic typesetting of computer printout. Although FORTRAN can be used for text processing, it is generally more cumbersome than PL/I or SNOBOL, especially in a classroom environment. The only advantage that FORTRAN might have over these two is the efficiency of the resulting program. This advantage is questionable in light of the relative programming ease that PL/I and SNOBOL provide.

The LISP language's principal uses lie in the area of formula manipulation. It is especially good for expressing recursive relations, and thus describing complex algebraic and logical patterns. However, the style of LISP is not conventional and somewhat difficult to assimilate without some prior experience in mathematical logic or recursive functions. Sedelow and Bobrow (62) report the use of LISP in 1964 to develop a program for stylistic analysis. No recent use of LISP in text processing is known by this writer, although it appears to have wider use in certain areas of artificial intelligence and theorem proving.

Many PL/I applications in text processing are reported in the literature. Martindale (43) describes LEXSTAT, a PL/I program for computing lexical statistics. PL/I has also been used successfully in the development of machine translation systems (76). PL/I's combined ability to manipulate both character string data and random access files is necessary for applications like machine translation. These two features are not usually found within a single programming language.

In spite of its usefulness for text processing, PL/I does not possess the extensive string manipulation power of SNOBOL. Some efforts to augment PL/I's string manipulation facilities, along the lines suggested in Section 2-7, have been reported in the literature. See, for example, the paper by Fink (23).

SNOBOL's string manipulation facilities are, as we have seen in Chapter 3, extensive. Its main limitations are its relatively restricted facilities for file manipulation and its lack of modern control structures for writing readable programs. Nevertheless, SNOBOL has enjoyed success both as a pedagogical tool and as a practical programming language. A paper by Wyatt (83) surveys the applications of SNOBOL in natural language research. One area of language research where SNOBOL is particularly well suited is the analysis of syntax. For example, a paper by Blackburn (8) discusses the use of SNOBOL for recursive description of generative grammars. In another paper, Elovitz *et al.* (22) describe the use of SNOBOL for translating English text to phonetics. The output is used in a speech synthesis system.

Thus, the use of different programming languages in text processing is extensive. For a more detailed evaluation of different languages' comparative strengths and weaknesses in text processing, see Tucker (75). Perhaps the most widely used language for text processing is machine level assembly language. For example, most interactive text editors are written in an assembly language because of its relative efficiency.

5-2.   Text Editing, Formatting, and Bibliographic Information Retrieval Packages

A wide range of activity has occurred in the use of packaged programs for text editing, formatting, and bibliographic information retrieval. In Chapter 4, we illustrated the use of the CMS Editor (15), SCRIPT (61), and FAMULUS (67) for these respective purposes. Our choice was dictated by convenience; these three packages happen to be available on the particular computer that the author is using at the present time, an IBM 370 with OS/VS1 and CMS, under VM/370.

Although this is a common computer configuration, there are many others. Moreover, most packages are developed specifically for use by a single computer and are not easily transported to another. For example, CMS, SCRIPT, and FAMULUS will run only on the IBM 360 or 370 computer. Other computers also have a collection of packages that are developed for them. The quality and variety of packages that are available differ widely from one computer to another. Understandably, the most extensively developed collection of software packages are those that run on the IBM 360 and 370 computers, since they have the widest usage.

It is our intention in this section to identify particular packages that are available for IBM and non-IBM computers. We also identify certain other publications that will help the reader to pursue the subject of text processing packages in more detail.

There are a number of interactive text editors in addition to CMS. Van Dam and Rice (77) have written an excellent, though now somewhat dated, survey of text editors. More recently, the National Technical Information Service has published an annotated bibliography on automated text editing (4). Nine different text editors and formatting packages are comparatively evaluated in a 1976 study by Riddle (56).

For the IBM 370 computer, there are other text editors in addition to CMS. For example, WYLBUR (84) is a text editor that allows full page editing and a number of other elaborate features that make it more attractive than CMS. However, WYLBUR requires more expensive terminals in order for its functions to be utilized. Other alternatives to CMS are EMILY (29), developed at Argonne National Laboratory and HES (13), an interactive editing and formatting package developed at the University of Illinois.

Most non-IBM computers have comparable text editing facilities available. For instance, the DEC PDP-10 has an editor known as TECO (74), or Text

Editor and Corrector. The CDC 7600 computers have an editing package known as TRIX AC (14), developed at Lawrence Livermore Laboratories. The UNIX time sharing operating system has an interactive editor known as NED (37).

Various minicomputers also have interactive text editing software. For example, Yule (85) reports a text editor for the Varian 620i. Schneider and Watts (60) describe SITAR, another on-line text processing system for minicomputers.

Some text editors are either part of a more ambitious package, or else have specialized uses. For example, TPS (5) is a batch-oriented text processing system for IBM OS/MVT operating systems. IRATE (41) is an interactive editor designed especially for complex technical text and structured data. TYPER (70) is designed especially for the one-line composition of text. Finally, LEXICO (78) is a complete text processing package that can be used in dictionary construction. In addition to a text editor, LEXICO has facilities for concordance generation, word classification, and generating dictionary entries. Its built-in defaults, interactive design, and simple language encourages nonprogrammers to exploit its capabilities.

Text formatting capabilities have been built into a variety of standalone computers for use in a field known as *word processing*. This field is active in the private sector, where there is a need for mass production of "personalized" correspondence. Increased use of text formatting has also occurred recently in the newspaper industry as an aid in the typesetting of news stories.

Text formatting software for medium and large computers has seen some use in the production of research manuscripts for publication and other teaching materials. Aside form SCRIPT, other text formatting packages are used with non-IBM computers. For example, TRIX RED (46) is a report editor for the CDC 7600 computer.

The principal use for bibliographic information retrieval packages occurs among individual students and researchers. Jahoda (36) has written a book that discusses the use of such packages in a university research environment. Another book, edited by Walker (79), addresses the user/computer interface in interactive bibliographic search. These references should be viewed as just the "tip of the iceberg" in a very broad field known as *information storage and retrieval*. The principal perspective of this field, however, is one of designing information retrieval systems rather than using them, and thus is beyond the scope of this book.

5-3   Concordance Generation Packages and Applications

The concordance generation program illustrated in Chapter 4 is known as GUKWIC (26), and was developed by Gnugnoli for the IBM 370 computer at Georgetown University. A large number of other concordance generation packages are in use as well. For example, Starkweather (72) describes a different concordance generator for the IBM computer. Ramus (55) describes another concordance generator known as CONCORD, which runs on a CDC 7600 computer.

Although the fundamental process of concordance generation is that which was illustrated in Chapter 4, different packages exhibit options that are more or less useful in special situations. A number of published articles discuss the use of these options, as well as the larger question of the proper use of concordances in linguistic and literary research (11, 21, 35, 39, 50). In addition to these, Crosland (17) discusses the particular use of the concordance in the study of the novel, and Gilbert (25) discusses automatic collation for medieval texts.

Literally hundreds of actual computer-generated concordances have been published. A small sampling of these are listed below:

Concordance	Reference
The Book of Isaiah, from the Bible	(54)
The Harvard Concordance to Shakespeare	(71)
Milton's *Paradise Lost*	(31)
The poems of Samuel Johnson	(47)

The author was unable to locate anything that resembles a complete index of computer-generated concordances. Such an index would appear to be a valuable contribution to the field.

5-4 Content Analysis, Machine Translation, and Other Research Areas

Beyond the concordance, a number of other computer-based methodologies have been developed as aids in literary and linguistic research. The most conspicuous developments at the present time are in the areas of content analysis, stylistic analysis, and machine translation.

Content analysis is a relatively young collection of methodologies for applying statistics to the analysis of text. The goal of such analysis is to determine or verify characteristics of randomly selected text, such as authorship, historical period of origin, and various social, political, or other characteristics of the period in which the text was written.

A computer program known as the General Inquirer (3, 73) is probably the most widely publicized content analysis package. Developed in the 1960s, the General Inquirer permits the researcher to develop a computer-based dictionary that serves to define categories and other characteristics for words in a text. It then allows the researcher to pass a text against this dictionary, and thus derive counts of the occurrences of all words in each of the predefined categories. These counts can then be analyzed statistically in order to draw various inferences about the original text. The Inquirer has been used in a number of content analysis projects. For example, Kelly and Stone have used it to identify different senses of English word usage (38).

Other content analysis programs, in addition to the Inquirer, have also been developed. For example, Meunier *et al.* (45) describe a system for text and content analysis. Iker and Klein (34) describe a package called WORDS, also designed for content analysis.

A number of other works are published that discuss the use of content analysis methodologies in language research. For example, Olney *et al.* (49) describe a technique for detecting patterns of term usage in text. Raben (52) examines content analysis in the study of poetry, and Danielson (18) and Schank (59) discuss the computer analysis of news prose.

For many years, substantial research effort has been made in the area of machine translation. Primitive systems were developed in the early 1960s, principally translating from Russian to English. Since then, efforts have been scattered and narrowly focused on particular problems inherent in machine translation systems. Log (42) has recently published an article entitled "Machine Translation: Past, Present, and Future," which serves as an overview of the subject. Other publications (16, 80) focus on the particular linguistic problems that are inherent in machine translation. Others emphasize the technical and programming aspects of implementing machine translation systems (76).

Special software accompanies a number of other research projects in text processing. For example, the use of the computer in stylistic analysis has been widely investigated (20, 53, 57, 64). Small and Koenig (69) have developed a technique that automatically classifies journal titles into fields or specialities. Compared with hand classification, this technique appears to be effective. Pratt and Silva have developed a procedure called PHONTRNS (51, 68), which automatically transcribes French text into phonetic symbols. Computer generation of braille from printed text has recently been reported by Fortier and Keeping (24). Finally, a system called REL (30) has been developed as a complete linguistic analysis tool. REL contains a syntax parser, a semantic processor, and additional facilities that aid in the analysis and synthesis of language structures.

5-5 Additional Bibliographies and Other Sources

We are able to present in this chapter only a small sample from among the numerous publications in the various areas of text processing. Moreover, the works referenced here will, soon after publication of this book, become outdated.

In this section, we can merely leave the reader with a "link to the past and future" by identifying additional sources of reference material that will continue to be refreshed and represent current developments in this fast-evolving field.

In 1971, IBM published two literature surveys (32, 33), which provide an excellent summary of progress in literary data processing and computers in the humanities up to that time, and which contain extensive bibliographies. Also, two surveys by Sedelow (63, 65) provide extensive bibliographic information on the use of the computer in language research in the 1960s and early 1970s. More recently, an NTIS bibliography (48) on natural language processing was published in 1978 and contains abstracts. Finally, a book by Dingwall (19), entitled *A Survey of Linguistic Science,* was also published in 1978.

Much information can also be found in books that are collections of papers, often selected proceedings of a conference, on text processing. For example, an early collection of papers on stylistic analysis and related topics was edited by Borko in 1967 (9). Another 1967 collection, edited by Bowles (10), is representative of the use of computers in humanistic research at that time. A 1971 collection (81) contains papers on concordance generation, stylistic analysis, and programming languages for humanists. In 1973, the proceedings of the International Conference on Computational Linguistics (87) was published. It contains papers on such topics as the automatic construction of indexes, computer archives, sentence paraphrasing from a conceptual base, syntactic and semantic analysis, speech understanding, and machine translation. Two other collections, published in 1973 (58) and 1977 (86), contain more articles on these topics. Together, such collections tend to be representative of the current state of development in text processing research.

A final source of ongoing information is found in several periodicals that regularly publish research papers in different areas of text processing. Notable among these periodicals are the following:

ALLC Bulletin (1),
American Journal of Computational Linguistics (2),
Bibliography and Subject Index to Current Computing Literature (6),
Language and Data Processing (40),
SIGLASH Newsletter (66).

5-6 Conclusion

We expect that this information will be helpful to the reader who wishes to further pursue some area of text processing. Text processing appears at present to be in its infancy; there is exciting and fruitful research to be done in all areas. Current programming languages, although adequate, are by no means ideal in their support for humanistic computing. Current packages, although widely used, are susceptible to dramatic enrichment in their functional capabilities. Much remains to be understood in the different areas of linguistic research: content analysis, machine translation, speech synthesis, and so forth. This book, therefore, should be taken very lightly; it characterizes some of the beginnings of text processing rather than an end. The best is yet to come!

Answers to Selected Exercises

Chapter 1

7. (a)

Step	Instruction	Text	Counter
1	1	GO .	$\boxed{0}$
2	2	GO .	
3	3	↑	
4	4		$\boxed{1}$
5	5		
6	2	GO .	
7	3	↑	
8	4		$\boxed{2}$
9	5		
10	2		
11	3 (stop)		

8.

Instruction number	Instruction
1.	Set the counter to zero.
2.	Move to the beginning of the next word.
3.	If there is no next word, stop.
4.	Otherwise, if the next word is "the," add 1 to the counter.
5.	Go to instruction number 2.

12. (a) Each 1000-character block and its trailing gap will take $1000/1600 + 0.75 = 0.625 + 0.75 = 1.375$ in. Each block contains $1000/6 = 166\frac{2}{3}$ words (including trailing blanks). Thus, 100,000 words will take $100,000/(1,000/6) = 600$ blocks, or 600×1.375 inches on the tape. This is 825 in. or about 68 ft, a small portion of a reel.

Chapter 2

2. (a) DCL I FIXED BIN;   (b) DCL NAME CHAR(20) VAR;
(c) DCL COST FIXED DEC (10,2);

4. DCL NAMES (100) CHAR (20) VAR;

5. (a) GET LIST (NAMES(1),NAMES(2));
(b) GET EDIT (NAMES(1),NAMES(2))(COL(10),A(20),COL(40),A(20));

6. (b) (i) 17.50, (ii) 17.52, (iii) −0.25

7. (b) (i) 'SUNbb', (ii) 'SUNNY', (iii) 'SUNNY'

8. (a) PUT EDIT (WORDS) (COL(1),A,COL(31),A,COL(61),A,COL(91),A);
(b) PUT EDIT (WORDS) (COL(53),A);
(c) PUT EDIT (WORDS(I) DO I = 4 TO 1 BY −1) (COL(1),A);

9. (a) H   24
AMT   06.2

10. (a) COUNTERS = 0;
(b) COUNTERS(4) = COUNTERS(1)+COUNTERS(2)+COUNTERS(3);

11. DCL COUNTERS(12) FIXED BIN INIT((12)0);

13. (a) IF S = T THEN I = I+1;   (c) IF A+B > B*C THEN I = I+1;

14. (a) COUNT = 0;
DO I = 1 TO 100;
IF WORDS (I = 'AN'| WORDS(I) = 'THE'| WORDS(I) = 'A'
THEN COUNT = COUNT+1;
END;

15. READER: PROC;
DCL CARD CHAR(80) STATIC;
ON ENDFILE (SYSIN) STOP;
GET EDIT (SENT) (A(80));
DO WHILE (INDEX(SENT,'.b')=0);
GET EDIT (CARD) (A(80));
SENT=SENT || CARD;
END;
END READER;

18. (a) 'THEREFORE, . . . THE' (b) 'THEbDOG' (c) 'THEREFORE'
(d) ' . . . THEREF'

19. (a) 'THEREFOR' (b) 'THEbDOGb'

21. (a) I = INDEX (SENT, 'THE');
DO WHILE (I⌐= 0);
CALL DELETE(SENT,İ,J);
I = INDEX(SENT, 'THE');
END;

Chapter 3

1. LOOP OUTPUT = INPUT :S(LOOP)F(END)

3. COUNTS = ARRAY<3,0>
* READ THE NEXT SENTENCE
NEXT S = TRIM(INPUT)   :F(PRINT)
* FIND NEXT WORD OR TOKEN IN S, AND DELETE IT FROM S
S SPAN('b') BREAK('b') . WORD = ''   :F (READ)

```
      I = 1
      WORD POS(0) ('A' | 'AN' | 'THE') RPOS(0)                    :S(FOUND)
      I = 2
      WORD POS(0) ANY('.?!') RPOS(0)                              :S(FOUND)
      I = 3
      WORD POS(0) ANY(':;(),-') RPOS(0)                   :S(FOUND)F(NEXT)
* INCREMENT COUNT WHEN FOUND
FOUND COUNTS(I) = COUNTS(I)+1                                     :(NEXT)
* PRINT RESULTS
PRINT OUTPUT = 'CLASS                 FREQUENCY'
      OUTPUT = 'ARTICLES           ' COUNTS<1>
      OUTPUT = 'SENTENCES          ' COUNTS<2>
      OUTPUT = 'OTHER PUNCTUATION  ' COUNTS<3>
END
```

4. (a) WORD ('S' | 'ED' | 'ING') RPOS(0)
   (b) WORD POS(0) 'DE' ARB 'ED' RPOS(0)
   (c) WORD ('DE' ARB 'ED') | ('ED' ARB 'DE')

5. Note that if two successive cards' contents are CARD1 and CARD2, a word is split between them if and only if (i) position 80 of CARD1 is nonblank, and (ii) position 1 of CARD2 is nonblank. The following pattern match statements will transfer to SPLIT when these conditions are true, and transfer to NEXT otherwise:

```
CARD1 NOTANY('ƀ') RPOS(0)  :F(NEXT)
CARD2 POS(0) NOTANY('ƀ')   :S(SPLIT)
NEXT
SPLIT
```

The split WORD itself can be captured from CARD1 and CARD2 as follows:

```
CARD1 SPAN(NOTANY('ƀ')) . W1 RPOS(0)
CARD2 BREAK('ƀ') . W2
WORD = W1 W2
```

The remainder of this exercise is left to the reader.

6. Here, we need only to strip the leading blanks from CARD1 as soon as it is read, and before looking for a split word.

7. A string S is an "ordinary word" if the following pattern match succeeds.

```
S POS(0)  SPAN(ALPHA) RPOS(0)
```

and the following pattern match fails:

```
S (POS(0) '-' ) | ('-' RPOS(0))
```

Here ALPHA = 'ABCDEFGHIJKLMNOPQRSTUVWXYZ'.

To eliminate repeated occurrences of each nonordinary word, say NONORD, an array named NONORDS can be kept that contains all such words that have been encountered so far. If N counts the number of these words, the following loop determines whether or not NONORD is already among the first N entries in NONORDS:

```
          I = 0
LOOP      I = LT(I,N) I+1            :F (NOTFOUND)
          IDENT(NONORD, NONORDS<I>)  :S (FOUND)F(LOOP)
FOUND
:
NOTFOUND
```

Note that if the word is NOTFOUND in the array, the value of I gives the next available location for adding it to the array. This is done simply as follows:

```
NOTFOUND    NONORDS<I> = NONORD
            N = N+1
```

8. DEFINE ('PLURAL(NOUN)')
```
    :
PLURAL NOUN 'Y' RPOS(0) = 'IES'                                    :S(RETURN)
NOUN DUPL(NOTANY('AEIOU'),2) RPOS(0) = NOUN 'ES'                   :S(RETURN)
NOUN = NOUN 'S'                                                    :(RETURN)
```

9. The invocation of PLURAL for 'FOLLY' is

```
S = PLURAL('FOLLY')
```

which will leave S = 'FOLLIES'.

10. Precede the text with the following control information:

```
.LL 30 ; .PL 42
```

Together with the default values for the top and bottom margins, this allows the text to be printed with 1-in. side margins, 30 lines per page, and 30 characters per line.

11. If S contains an input line of text, then the following statement will identify a *leading* occurrence of 'Ab' in S followed by '.b' and insert '#HEADING#b' between them:

```
S POS(0) (SPAN('b') | ") 'Ab') . T '.b' = T '#HEADING#b.b'
```

The following statement will identify any other occurrence of 'bAb' in S, and insert '#ARTICLE#b' after it:

```
S 'bAb' NOTANY('.') . T = 'bAb#ARTICLE#b' T
```

CHAPTER 4

2. For pedagogical and practical purposes, assume that the text contains no more than 1000 words, and for each word save only 30 characters of left context and 30 characters or right context. A word can be assumed to be no more than 20 characters long, so that the basic array for the concordance will require 80,000 storage locations (at most). For larger text, an auxiliary file should be used, together with a file sorting package, in order to get the words into alphabetical sequence.

3. Here, the storage requirements are not as great as in question 2. For each word, only a frequency counter needs to be saved rather than its context.

4. (a) Use the GALLEY program, with the following control cards:

```
/ID/TEXT PROCESSING BIBLIOGRAPHY
/FIELDS/(TI,DATE)
/PRINT BY FIELDS/
```

(b) Use the EDIT program, with the following control cards:

```
/ID/TEXT PROCESSING BIBLIOGRAPHY
/REPLACE/(1-5)(DATE)*b19*b'*
```

(c) Use the SORT program, together with the following control cards:

```
/ID/TEXT PROCESSING BIBLIOGRAPHY
/FIELDS/(DATE,TI)
```

(d) Use the SEARCH program, together with the following control cards:

```
/ID/TEXT PROCESSING BIBLIOGRAPHY
/SEARCH/(TEXT(TI) | STRING(TI)) & 197(DATE)
```

APPENDIX A

EBCDIC and ASCII Character Sets

Following are listed the characters in the standard EBCDIC and ASCII character sets For each character we give its punched card code and its hexadecimal or octal representation. The punched card code is given as a combination of punches in the 12 rows, or vertical positions, within each of the 80 positions in a punched card (see Fig. 1–7).

The top two rows in the card are known as the 12 and 11 rows, respectively. The remaining ten rows are numbered 0 through 9 respectively, as indicated in Fig. 1–7. The hexadecimal (hex) or octal representation refers to each character's internal form when it is stored in a computer. The choice between hex and octal depends upon the particular computer in use. (Some special characters in the EBCDIC and ASCII character sets are omitted from this list, due to their infrequent use.)

EBCDIC character	Punched card code	Hex representation	EBCDIC character	Punched card code	Hex representation	EBCDIC character	Punched card code	Hex representation
ƀ	(no punches)	40	#	3-8	7B	0	0	F0
¢	12-2-8	4A	@	4-8	7C	1	1	F1
.	12-3-8	4B	'	5-8	7D	2	2	F2
<	12-4-8	4C	=	6-8	7E	3	3	F3
(	12-5-8	4D	"	7-8	7F	4	4	F4
+	12-6-8	4E	a	12-0-1	81	5	5	F5
|	12-7-8	4F	⋯	⋯	⋯	6	6	F6
&	12	50	i	12-0-9	89	7	7	F7
!	11-2-8	5A	j	12-11-1	91	8	8	F8
$	11-3-8	5B	⋯	⋯	⋯	9	9	F9
*	11-4-8	5C	r	12-11-9	99			
)	11-5-8	5D	s	11-0-2	A2			
;	11-6-8	5E	⋯	⋯	⋯			
¬	11-7-8	5F	A	12-1	C1			
-	11	60	⋯	⋯	⋯			
/	0-1	61	I	12-9	C9			
,	0-3-8	6B	J	11-1	D1			
%	0-4-8	6C	⋯	⋯	⋯			
_	0-5-8	6D	R	11-9	D9			
>	0-6-8	6E	S	0-2	E2			
?	0-7-8	6F	⋯	⋯	⋯			
:	2-8	7A						

ASCII character	Punched card code	Octal representation
ƀ	11-0-1-8-9	40
!	0-1-9	41
"	0-2-9	42
#	0-3-9	43
$	0-4-9	44
%	0-5-9	45
&	0-6-9	46
'	0-7-9	47
(	0-8-9	50
)	0-1-8-9	51
*	0-2-8-9	52
+	0-3-8-9	53
,	0-4-8-9	54
|	0-5-8-9	55
.	0-6-8-9	56
/	0-7-8-9	57
0	12-11-0-1-8-9	60
1	1-9	61
2	2-9	62
3	3-9	63
4	4-9	64
5	5-9	65
6	6-9	66
7	7-9	67
8	8-9	70
9	1-8-9	71
:	2-8-9	72
;	3-8-9	73
<	4-8-9	74
=	5-8-9	75
>	6-8-9	76
?	7-8-9	77
@	(no punches)	100
A	12-0-1-9	101
...	...	...
H	12-0-8-9	110
I	12-1-8	111
...	...	...
O	12-7-8	117
P	12	120
Q	12-11-1-9	121
...	...	...
X	12-11-8-9	130
Y	11-1-8	131
Z	11-2-8	132
[	11-3-8	133
\	11-4-8	134
]	11-5-8	135
⌐	11-6-8	136
‾	11-7-8	137
`	11	140
a	0-1	141
b	11-0-2-9	142
...	...	...
h	11-0-8-9	150
i	0-1-8	151
j	12-11	152
k	0-3-8	153
...	...	...
o	0-7-8	157
p	12-11-0	160
q	12-11-0-1-9	161
...	...	...
x	12-11-0-8-9	170
y	1-8	171
z	2-8	172
|	4-8	174

APPENDIX B

Selected Conventions for Tape and Disk I/O

In order to read or write text data on magnetic tape or magnetic disk, certain additional "control" information must be supplied. This information differs from one computer to the next, and is typically not part of a high-level programming language like PL/I or SNOBOL. To illustrate what is involved with tape and disk I/O, we include here some selected illustrations using PL/I on the IBM 370 computer. This choice of computer and language is made strictly on the basis of convenience to the author.

To create a copy on tape or disk from a text file that is stored on another medium, such as punched cards, the following general program structure and control information can be used:

```
P: PROC OPTIONS (MAIN);
   DCL COPY FILE RECORD OUTPUT, CARD
       CHAR (80);
   ON ENDFILE (SYSIN) STOP;
   DO WHILE ('1'B);
       GET EDIT (CARD) (A(80));
       WRITE FILE(COPY) FROM(CARD);
       END;
   END P;

/*
//GO.SYSIN DD *
       Cards to be copied
   /*
```

160

```
//GO.COPY DD DSNAME=COPYFILE,UNIT= | TAPE  |
                                   | SYSDA |  ,
//  VOL=SER=serial#,DISP=(NEW,KEEP),
//   DCB=(RECFM=FB,LRECL=80, BLKSIZE=1600)
```

Here, the name of the tape file is COPY, and a record is written to it by using the statement

```
WRITE FILE(COPY) FROM(CARD);
```

To define the particular format, or layout, of the file on tape or disk, the three control lines at the bottom of this example are needed.

The syntax of this control information is more rigid and obtuse than that of PL/I. The language in which it is written is called *job control language,* or JCL. To select tape or disk as the medium for this file write UNIT=TAPE or UNIT=SYSDA on the first control card. To identify the particular tape reel or disk pack to be used, give the "serial#" as shown on the second control card. The last control card essentially identifies that the records on tape will be 80 characters long (LRECL=80), they will be blocked (RECFM=FB), and each block will contain 1600 characters (BLKSIZE=1600).

To read this same file from tape or disk and, say, list its contents, the following general program structure and control information can be used:

```
    Q: PROC OPTIONS (MAIN);
       DCL AFILE FILE RECORD INPUT, CARD CHAR(80);
       ON ENDFILE (AFILE) STOP;
       DO WHILE ('1'B);
          READ FILE (AFILE) INTO(CARD);
          PUT SKIP EDIT (CARD) (A(80));
          END;
    END Q;
/*
// GO.AFILE DD DSNAME=COPYFILE,UNIT= | SYSDA |
                                     | TAPE  |  ,
// VOL=SER=serial#, DISP = OLD
```

Here, the file must be accessed by the same name (DSNAME = COPYFILE) and the same UNIT (=TAPE or =SYSDA) under which it had been created, and the serial# must be specified as well. Notice that the third control card is not required for a tape or disk *input* file, since the record and block sizes were made known to the system when the file was created.

These examples are very brief. They assume that the tape and disk files are supplied with standard labels, for instance, and take advantage of that situation. For more detailed information on this subject, the reader is advised to consult his/her computer center.

APPENDIX C

Glossary of Text Processing Primitives

The following list identifies the different functions, or *primitives,* upon which many text processing applications are based. Each of these is discussed in one or more chapters throughout the book. Here, we briefly define each primitive and indicate the chapter(s) where it is discussed.

Bibliographic creation:	The preparation of entries in a bibliography file in a form that can be processed by computer (Chapters 2 and 4)
Bibliographic search:	The random retrieval of information from a computer-based bibliographic file, in accordance with specific search criteria, such as date of publication (Chapters 2 and 4)
Concordance generation:	The alphabetical listing of every occurrence of each different word that occurs within a text, together with its immediate left and right context (Chapters 4 and 5)
Dictionary maintenance:	The addition and correction of selected entries in a computer-based dictionary (Chapter 2)
Dictionary search:	The random access of an individual entry (word or phrase) in a computer-based dictionary (Chapter 2)
Editing:	See Text editing
Formatting:	See Text formatting
Frequency counts:	Tabulation of the number of occurrences of each different word, word class, phrase, sentence, or other token within a computer-based text (Chapters 1, 2, 3, and 4)
Interactive text editing:	See Text editing
KWIC (key word in context) index:	See Concordance generation
List search:	The serial search of a list to determine whether or not a particular item is present (Chapter 2)

Paragraph formatting:	See Text formatting
Pattern matching:	The systematic examination of a text to determine whether or not its constituent parts conform to a particular pattern (Chapters 2 and 3)
Sorting:	The rearrangement of words in a text into alphabetical order (Chapters 1, 2, and 4)
Text editing:	The performance of insertions, changes, and deletions within a computer-based text. This is usually done through an interactive terminal (Chapters 1, 4, and 5)
Text formatting:	The detailed layout of computer-based text on a printed page for publication, including left and right margin alignment, page numbering, footnote placement, and automatic generation of indexes (Chapters 1, 3, and 4)
Word counting:	See Frequency counts
Word extraction:	The automatic extraction of words from a text, for purposes of frequency counts, sorting, concordance generation, and so forth (Chapters 1, 2, and 3)

References

1. *ALLC Bull.* Association for Literary and Linguistic Computing, 1973–.
2. *Amer. J. Computational Linguistics,* 1975–.
3. Arp, D. J., *et al.,* "An introduction to the Inquirer II system of content analysis," *Comput. Studies in the Humanities and Verbal Behavior* **3** (1970): 40-45.
4. *Automated Text Editing—A Bibliography with Abstracts,* PS-76/0181/8WAY, National Technical Information Service, Springfield, Virginia, 1976.
5. Barksdale, G. L., Jr., and Meyer, W. B., "TPS, a text processing system—Primer and reference manual," AD-A021-763/8ST, National Technical Information Service, Springfield, Virginia, 1976.
6. *Bibliography and Subject Index to Current Computing Literature,* Association for Computing Machinery, 1966.
7. Bingham, H. W., "Text editing using APL/700," *APL 76 Proc.,* ACM, New York (1976): 78-82.
8. Blackburn, J. D., "On generative grammar analysis: Recursion in SNOBOL," *ALLC Bull.* **4** (3) (1976): 221–222.
9. Borko, H., ed., *Automated Language Processing,* Wiley, New York, 1967.
10. Bowles, E. A., ed., *Computers in Humanistic Research,* Prentice-Hall, Englewood Cliffs, New Jersey, 1967.
11. Burton, D. M., "Some uses of a grammatical concordance," *Computers in the Humanities* **2** (1968): 145–154.
12. Carbrey, B., "A set of FORTRAN subroutines and function for character manipulation," AD-A040-207/3ST, National Technical Information Service, Springfield, Virginia, 1977.
13. Carmody, S., *et al.,* "A hypertext editing system for the /360," *Pertinent Concepts in Computer Graphics,* pp. 291–330, Univ. of Illinois Press, Carbondale, 1969.
14. Cecil, A., Mall, H. and Rinde, J., "TRIX AC: A set of general purpose text editing commands," UCID-30040, Lawrence Livermore Laboratory, Livermore, California, 1976.
15. *CMS: A Conversational Context-Directed Editor,* IBM Cambridge Scientific Center Report 320-2041, Cambridge, Massachusetts, 1969.
16. Crawford, T. D., "Project BABEL: Machine translation with English as the target language,"

in *The Computer in Literary and Linguistics Studies* (A. Jones and R. Churchhouse, eds.), Univ. of Wales Press, 1976.

17. Crosland, A. T., "The concordance and the study of the novel," *ALLC Bull.* **3** (1975): 190–196.

18. Danielson, W. A., "Computer analysis of news prose," *Computer Studies in the Humanities and Verbal Behavior* **1** (1968): 55–60.

19. Dingwall, W. O., *A Survey of Linguistic Science,* 2nd ed., Greylock Publishers, Stamford, Connecticut, 1978.

20. Donow, H. S., "Prosody and the computer: A text processor for stylistic analysis," *AFIPS Proc.* **36** (1970): 287–295.

21. Duggan, J. J., "The value of computer-generated concordances in linguistic and literary research," *Revue* **4** (1966): 51–60.

22. Elovitz, H. S., *et al.,* "Automatic translation of English text to phonetics by means of letter-to-sound rules," AD-A021-929/5ST, National Technical Information Service, Springfield, Virginia, 1976.

23. Fink, J., "Four PL/I subroutines for natural language processing," *SIGLASH Newsletter* **9** (3) (1976): 12–19.

24. Fortier, P. A., and Keeping, D., "The University of Manitoba computer braille project," *Third Internat. Conf. on Computing in the Humanities, Pisa.,* pp. 265–271, 1977.

25. Gilbert, P., "Automatic collation: A technique for medieval texts," *Computers in the Humanities* **7** (1973): 139–147.

26. Gnugnoli, G., *Introduction to GUKWIC,* Georgetown Univ. Press, Washington, D.C., 1972.

27. Hammer, D. P., "Problems in the conversion of bibliographic data—A keypunching experiment," *Amer. Documentation* 19 (1968): 12–17.

28. Hann, M., "On the adaption of ALGOL for linguistic programming," *Internat. Rev. Appl. Linguistics* **32** (1976): 57–72.

29. Hansen, W. J., "Creation of hierarchic text with a computer display," Argonne National Lab ANL7818, Argonne, Illinois, 1971.

30. Heinsz-Dostert, B., and Thompson, F. B., "The REL system and REL English," *Computational Math. Linguistics* **12** (1973): 533–555.

31. Hudson, G. W., *Paradise Lost: A Concordance,* Gale Research, Detroit, 1970.

32. IBM, *Introduction to Computers in the Humanities,* White Plains, New York, 1971.

33. IBM, *Literary Data Processing,* White Plains, New York, 1971.

34. Iker, H. P., and Klein, R., "Words: A computer system for the analysis of content." *Behavioral Research Methods and Instrumentation* **6** (1974): 430–438.

35. Ingram, W., "Concordances in the seventies," *Computers in the Humanities* **8** (1974): 273–277.

36. Jahoda, M., *Information Storage and Retrieval Systems for Individual Researchers,* Wiley, New York, 1970.

37. Kelly, J., "A guide to NED: A new on-line computer editor," Rand Corp. Rpt. #R2000-ARPA, Santa Monica, California, 1977.

38. Kelly, E., and Stone, P. J., *Computer Recognition of English Word Senses,* North-Holland Publ. Co., Amsterdam, 1975.

39. Koubourlis, D. J., "On concordances and their uses," *Slavic and East European J.* **19** (1975): 246–253.

40. *Language and Data Processing,* Max Niemeyer Verlag, Tübingen, Germany.

41. Leavitt, M., and Lederer, C. M., "Overview of IRATE: An interactive retrieval system and text editor," LBL-4607, National Technical Information Service, Springfield, Virginia, 1975.

42. Log, S. C., "Machine translation: Past, present, and future," *ALLC Bull.* **4** (1976): 105–114.

43. Martindale, C. A., "LEXSTAT: A PL/I program for computation of lexical statistics," *Behavior Res. Meth. Instrum.* **6** (1974): 571.

44. Messina, C. G., and Hilsenrath, J., "Edit-insertion programs for automatic typesetting of computer printout," PB-191-352, National Technical Information Service, Springfield, Virginia, 1970.
45. Meunier, J. G., *et al.*, "A system for text and content analysis," *Computers in the Humanities* **10** (1976): 281–286.
46. Moll, H., "TRIX RED: A report editor for the CDC 7600," UCID-30142, Lawrence Livermore Laboratory, Livermore, California, 1976.
47. Nangle, H. H., ed., *A Concordance to the Poems of Samuel Johnson,* Cornell Univ. Press, Ithaca, New York, 1973.
48. *Natural Language Processing* (Bibliography with Abstracts), NTIS,PS-78/1312, 1978.
49. Olney, J., *et al.*, "A new technique for detecting patterns of term usage in text corpora," *Information Processing Management,* **12** (1976): 235–250.
50. Peavler, J. M., "Analysis of corpora of variations," *Computers in the Humanities* **8** (1974): 153–159.
51. Pratt, B., and Silva, G., *PHONTRNS: A procedure which uses a computer for transcribing French text into phonetic symbols,* Clayton, Victoria, Australia, 1967.
52. Raben, J. A., "Content analysis and the study of poetry", in *The Analysis of Communication Content,* (George Gerbner *et al.*, eds.), pp. 175–186, Wiley, New York, 1969.
53. Raben, J. A., "Computer/stylistics seminar: A report," *Computers in the Humanities* **3** (1969): 209-210.
54. Radday, Y. T., *An Analytical Linguistic Concordance to the Book of Isaiah,* Biblical Research Associates, Wooster, Ohio, 1971.
55. Ramus, J. E., "CONCORD: A word index generator for arbitrary text strings," UCID-30126, National Technical Information Service, Springfield, Virginia, 1975.
56. Riddle, E. A., "Comparative study of various text editors and formatting systems," AD-A029-050/2ST, National Technical Information Service, Springfield, Virginia, 1976.
57. Ross, D., Jr., and Rasche, R. S., "EYEBALL: A computer program for description of style," *Computers in the Humanities* **6** (1972): 213–221.
58. Rustin, R., ed., *Natural Language Processing,* Algorithmics Press, New York, 1973.
59. Schank, R. C., "Research at Yale in natural language processing," Tech. Rep. RR-84, Yale Univ., New Haven, Connecticut, 1976.
60. Schneider, B. R., Jr., and Watts, R. M., "SITAR: An interactive text processing system for small computers," *Comm. ACM* **20** (1977) 495–499.
61. *SCRIPT Reference Guide,* Univ. of Waterloo, Waterloo, Ohio, 1977.
62. Sedelow, S. Y., and Bobrow, D. B., "A LISP program for use in stylistic analysis," Systems Development Corp. Rpt #TM-1753, Santa Monica, California, 1964.
63. Sedelow, S. Y., "The computer in the humanities and fine arts," *Comput. Surveys* **2** (1970): 89-110.
64. Sedelow, S. Y., "The use of the computer for stylistic studies of Shakespeare," *Computer Studies in the Humanities and Verbal Behavior* **4** (1973): 33–36.
65. Sedelow, S. Y., and Sedelow, Walter A. Jr., *Language Research and the Computer,* Univ. of Kansas Press, Lawrence, Kansas, 1972.
66. *SIGLASH Newsletter,* Association for Computing Machinery, New York, 1968–.
67. Shaw, A., *Famulus Users Manual,* Univ. College London Computer Centre, London, 1972.
68. Silva, G., "PHONTRNS: An automatic orthographic-to-phonetic conversion systems for French," *Computers in the Humanities* **3** (1969): 257–265.
69. Small, H. G., and Koenig, E. D., "Journal clustering using a bibliographic coupling method," *Information Processing Management* **13** (1977): 277–288.
70. Sonderegger, R. P. Jr., "Typer: An editor for the on-line composition of text," *Proc. 3rd Annu. Conf on Computers, Communications, Graphics, Interactive Technology and Image Processing,* pp. 1–6, ACM, New York, 1976.

71. Spevack, M. (compiler), *The Harvard Concordance to Shakespeare,* Harvard Univ. Press, Cambridge, Massachusetts, 1974.

72. Starkweather, J.A., "A KWIC concordance generator," SHARE Document 360DO3.3.002.

73. Stone, P. J., *et al.,* eds., *The General Inquirer: A Computer Approach to Content Analysis,* MIT Press, Cambridge, Massachusetts, 1966.

74. *TECO: Text Editor and Corrector Reference Manual,* Interactive Sciences Corp., Braintree, Massachusetts, 1969.

75. Tucker, A. B., *Programming Langauages,* McGraw-Hall, New York, 1977.

76. Tucker, A. B., Gnugnoli, G, Nguyen, L., and Chaloupka, B., "Implementation considerations for machine translation," *Proc. ACM 78* **2** (1978): 884–890.

77. Van Dam, A., and Rice, D., "On-line text editing: A survey," *Computing Surveys* **3** (1971): 93–114.

78. Venezky, R.L., *et al.,* "User aids in a lexical processing system," *3rd Internat. Conf. on Computing in the Humanities,* pp. 317–325, Univ. of Waterloo Press, 1977.

79. Walker, D. E., ed., *Interactive Bibliographic Search: The User/Computer Interface,* AFIPS, Montvale, New Jersey, 1971.

80. Wilks, Y., *Grammar, Meaning, and the Machine Analysis of Language,* Routledge and K. Paul, London, 1972.

81. Wisbey, R. A., ed., *The Computer in Literary and Linguistic Research,* Cambridge Univ. Press, London, 1971.

82. Woods, W. A. "Research in natural language understanding," Rep. BBN-3797, Cambridge, Massachusetts, 1978.

83. Wyatt, J. L., "SNOBOL applications in natural language research," *SIGLASH Newsletter* **8** (1975): 12–21.

84. *WYLBUR Reference Manual,* Stanford Univ. Press, Stanford California, 1970.

85. Yule, H. P., "Conversational text editor for a laboratory minicomputer," *Anal. Chem.,* **44** (1972): 430.

86. Zampoli, A., ed., *Linguistic Structures Processing,* North-Holland, Publ. Co., Amsterdam, 1977.

87. Zampoli, A., and Calzolan, N., eds., *Computational and Mathematical Linguistics, Proc. Internat. Conf. on Computational Linguistics,* Pisa, 1973.

Index

169

Computer Science and Applied Mathematics

A SERIES OF MONOGRAPHS AND TEXTBOOKS

Editor
Werner Rheinboldt
University of Maryland

HANS P. KÜNZI, H. G. TZSCHACH, and C. A. ZEHNDER. Numerical Methods of Mathematical Optimization: With ALGOL and FORTRAN Programs, Corrected and Augmented Edition

AZRIEL ROSENFELD. Picture Processing by Computer

JAMES ORTEGA AND WERNER RHEINBOLDT. Iterative Solution of Nonlinear Equations in Several Variables

AZARIA PAZ. Introduction to Probabilistic Automata

DAVID YOUNG. Iterative Solution of Large Linear Systems

ANN YASUHARA. Recursive Function Theory and Logic

JAMES M. ORTEGA. Numerical Analysis: A Second Course

G. W. STEWART. Introduction to Matrix Computations

CHIN-LIANG CHANG AND RICHARD CHAR-TUNG LEE. Symbolic Logic and Mechanical Theorem Proving

C. C. GOTLIEB AND A. BORODIN. Social Issues in Computing

ERWIN ENGELER. Introduction to the Theory of Computation

F. W. J. OLVER. Asymptotics and Special Functions

DIONYSIOS C. TSICHRITZIS AND PHILIP A. BERNSTEIN. Operating Systems

ROBERT R. KORFHAGE. Discrete Computational Structures

PHILIP J. DAVIS AND PHILIP RABINOWITZ. Methods of Numerical Integration

A. T. BERZTISS. Data Structures: Theory and Practice, Second Edition

N. CHRISTOPHIDES. Graph Theory: An Algorithmic Approach

ALBERT NIJENHUIS AND HERBERT S. WILF. Combinatorial Algorithms

AZRIEL ROSENFELD AND AVINASH C. KAK. Digital Picture Processing

SAKTI P. GHOSH. Data Base Organization for Data Management

DIONYSIOS C. TSICHRITZIS AND FREDERICK H. LOCHOVSKY. Data Base Management Systems

JAMES L. PETERSON. Computer Organization and Assembly Language Programming

WILLIAM F. AMES. Numerical Methods for Partial Differential Equations, Second Edition

ARNOLD O. ALLEN. Probability, Statistics, and Queueing Theory: With Computer Science Applications

ELLIOTT I. ORGANICK, ALEXANDRA I. FORSYTHE, AND ROBERT P. PLUMMER. Programming Language Structures

ALBERT NIJENHUIS AND HERBERT S. WILF. Combinatorial Algorithms. Second edition.

JAMES S. VANDERGRAFT. Introduction to Numerical Computations

AZRIEL ROSENFELD. Picture Languages, Formal Models for Picture Recognition